Buying Your First House
A Comprehensive Guide to Navigating the Journey of home ownership

Table of Contents

Introduction
1. The Exciting Journey Ahead
   - Setting Your Goals and Expectations
   - Understanding the Importance of home ownership

Chapter 1: Assessing Your Financial Readiness
   - Evaluating Your Credit Score
   - Budgeting for Your First Home
   - Saving for a Down Payment and Closing Costs
   - Managing Debt and Financial Responsibilities

Chapter 2: Finding the Right Real Estate Agent
   - The Role of a Real Estate Agent
   - How to Choose the Right Agent for You
   - Interviewing Potential Agents
   - Building a Trusting Relationship

Chapter 3: Navigating the Real Estate Market
   - Types of Properties
   - Understanding Market Trends
   - Determining Your Preferred Location
   - Online and Offline Property Searches

Chapter 4: Getting Pre-Approved for a Mortgage
   - The Importance of Mortgage Pre-Approval
   - Preparing Your Financial Documents
   - Comparing Mortgage Options
   - Understanding Interest Rates

Chapter 5: The House-Hunting Process
   - The First Viewing
   - Keeping an Open Mind
   - Making an Offer
   - Negotiating the Deal

Chapter 6: The Home Inspection
   - The Purpose of a Home Inspection
   - Finding a Qualified Home Inspector
   - Common Issues Found in Home Inspections
   - Negotiating Repairs and Credits

Chapter 7: Finalizing Your Mortgage
   - The Mortgage Application Process
   - Appraisal and Underwriting

- Closing Costs and Loan Documents
- Closing Day and Signing Your Mortgage

Chapter 8: home ownership Responsibilities
- Setting Up Utilities and Services
- Home Maintenance and Repairs
- Insurance and Property Taxes
- Planning for Future Upgrades

Chapter 9: Moving In and Making It Yours
- Preparing for the Move
- Unpacking and Organizing
- Personalizing Your New Home
- Getting to Know Your Neighborhood

Chapter 10: Navigating Challenges and Celebrating Success
- Dealing with Unexpected Issues
- Building Community and Relationships
- Achieving Your Long-Term home ownership Goals
- Celebrating Your home ownership Journey

Conclusion
- Reflecting on Your Journey
- Planning for Your Future in Your New Home
- Paying It Forward: Helping Others on Their Path to home ownership

Bonus Tips

In "Buying Your First House: A Comprehensive Guide to Navigating the Journey of home ownership," we will take you on a detailed and personal journey through the exciting process of buying your first home. From assessing your financial readiness to finding the right real estate agent, navigating the real estate market, and finally stepping into your new home, this book is designed to be your trusted companion every step of the way.

Throughout the chapters, we'll share personal anecdotes, expert advice, and practical tips to help you make informed decisions. Whether you're a first-time buyer or simply looking to refresh your knowledge, this book will empower you with the knowledge and confidence you need to make your dream of home ownership a reality. Welcome to the world of home ownership!

The Exciting Journey Ahead

Congratulations! You've taken the first step towards embarking on an exhilarating adventure – the journey to becoming a homeowner. The decision to buy your first house is a monumental one, filled with anticipation, dreams, and countless possibilities. As you stand at this crossroads, you're about to embark on a path that will not only provide you with a place to call your own but also offer you a canvas upon which to paint the story of your life.

This journey is not just about four walls and a roof; it's about creating a sanctuary, a place of refuge where you can build memories, raise a family, and express your unique personality. It's a financial investment that can provide stability, security, and, if done right, even financial growth. But more than that, it's an emotional investment in your future, a symbol of your hard work and aspirations.

In the pages of this book, we'll walk hand in hand through every stage of this journey, offering guidance, insights, and personal anecdotes to make your path smoother and more enjoyable. Along the way, we'll tackle questions you might have, address common concerns, and share stories of those who have successfully navigated this exciting adventure.

Remember that every home-buying experience is unique, and there will be moments of joy, uncertainty, and even challenges. But rest assured, the journey ahead is filled with the promise of new beginnings and the satisfaction of achieving one of life's most significant milestones.

So, fasten your seatbelt, because you're about to embark on a rollercoaster of emotions and experiences as you explore the world of real estate, navigate the financial intricacies, make important decisions, and finally, step over the threshold of your very own home. Get ready for "Buying Your First House" to be your trusted companion throughout this remarkable journey, offering guidance, support, and inspiration as you make your dream of home ownership a reality. Welcome to the exciting adventure that lies ahead!

Setting Your Goals and Expectations

Before you dive headfirst into the world of buying your first house, it's essential to set clear goals and manage your expectations. This chapter is like setting the coordinates on your GPS before embarking on a road trip – it helps you stay on course and avoid unnecessary detours.

1. Defining Your Goals:
   - Begin by asking yourself, "Why do I want to buy a house?" Is it for stability, investment, or to have a place to call your own?
   - Consider your long-term plans. Are you looking for a starter home, or is this a place where you envision yourself growing old?
   - Think about location. Are you looking to stay in your current city, or is this an opportunity to explore new horizons?
   - Factor in your lifestyle. Do you need a spacious backyard for your dog, or do you prefer a low-maintenance condo?
   - Assess your financial situation realistically. What can you comfortably afford, and what compromises are you willing to make?

2. Understanding Your Expectations:
   - Be prepared for a mix of emotions. Buying a house can be a rollercoaster ride with moments of excitement, frustration, and uncertainty.
   - Keep in mind that your first home may not be your forever home. It's okay if it doesn't meet all your dream home criteria.
   - Know that the process takes time. Finding the right house, securing financing, and closing the deal can take several months.
   - Be flexible and open to compromises. Rarely does a house check every box on your wish list.
   - Understand the financial commitment. home ownership comes with expenses beyond the mortgage, such as property taxes, insurance, and maintenance.

3. Setting Realistic Timelines:
   - Establish a timeline that aligns with your goals. Are you in a rush to move, or can you take your time to find the perfect home?
   - Be patient. The right house may not appear immediately, and it's okay to explore multiple options before making a decision.
   - Understand that the home-buying process involves several stages, each with its own timeline. From searching for properties to closing the deal, plan for each step accordingly.

4. Creating a Vision Board:
   - Visualize your dream home. Collect images, magazine clippings, or create a digital vision board to help clarify what you're looking for.
   - Share your vision with your real estate agent. They can better assist you when they have a clear understanding of your preferences.

Setting your goals and expectations is like laying a strong foundation for your house-hunting journey. It ensures that you're moving forward with a clear sense of purpose and an understanding of the challenges and triumphs that lie ahead. As you continue reading this book and proceed on your path to home ownership, keep these goals and expectations in mind, and let them guide you towards making informed decisions that align with your aspirations.

Understanding the Importance of home ownership

home ownership is more than just owning a piece of property; it's a milestone that carries significant personal, financial, and emotional importance. In this chapter, we will delve into the multifaceted aspects of home ownership and explore why it holds such a special place in the hearts and lives of many.

1. Financial Stability and Wealth Building:
   - home ownership is often seen as a cornerstone of financial stability. Paying a mortgage builds equity, which can be an asset for future endeavors or emergencies.
   - Historically, real estate has appreciated over time, making home ownership a potential avenue for long-term wealth building.
   - home ownership can offer tax benefits, such as deductions for mortgage interest and property taxes, which can positively impact your overall financial situation.

2. Personal and Emotional Fulfillment:
   - Owning a home provides a sense of permanence and stability. It's a place where you can create

lasting memories, raise a family, and establish roots in a community.
   - Personalization: Unlike renting, homeowners have the freedom to decorate, renovate, and modify their space to suit their preferences and needs.
   - Pride of Ownership: There's a unique sense of accomplishment that comes with owning your home. It represents your hard work and achievement.

3. Control and Independence:
   - home ownership grants you greater control over your living environment. You can make decisions about the property without seeking approval from a landlord.
   - It offers a degree of independence and self-sufficiency, allowing you to manage your living space on your terms.

4. Community and Social Ties:
   - Owning a home often fosters a stronger connection to the community. You're more likely to engage with neighbors and participate in local events and activities.
   - Being a homeowner can provide stability for children, allowing them to attend the same schools and build lasting friendships.

5. Retirement Planning:
   - Many people view their homes as part of their retirement strategy. Once the mortgage is paid off, housing costs decrease, freeing up more funds for retirement savings or other pursuits.
   - Downsizing is a common strategy for retirees, allowing them to unlock equity and potentially reduce living expenses.

6. Sense of Belonging:
   - home ownership often leads to a deeper sense of belonging. You become an integral part of a neighborhood and contribute to its overall character and vitality.

7. Investment in the Future:
   - Your home can serve as a legacy for future generations, providing a place for your family to gather and create their own memories.
   - home ownership allows you to leave a lasting mark on the world, whether through property improvements, community involvement, or even environmental sustainability efforts.

While home ownership comes with responsibilities and financial commitments, it offers a wide array of benefits that extend far beyond the tangible aspects of property ownership. Understanding the importance of home ownership can help you appreciate the journey you are about to embark upon and motivate you to make informed decisions as you pursue your dream of owning your first house.

Chapter 1: Assessing Your Financial Readiness

In the exhilarating journey of buying your first house, few chapters are as crucial as this one. "Assessing Your Financial Readiness" is where the rubber meets the road, where dreams take shape, and reality sets in. It's the moment when you evaluate your financial situation to determine whether you're ready to take this significant step towards home ownership.

While the allure of owning a home is undeniable, it's essential to recognize that it comes with financial responsibilities and commitments. The decision to buy a house involves careful consideration of your current financial standing, budgeting skills, and long-term financial goals. In this chapter, we will guide you through the process of assessing your financial readiness to ensure that you embark on this journey well-prepared and informed.

The Roadmap Ahead:

1. Evaluating Your Credit Score: Your credit score is a vital piece of the home ownership puzzle. We will explore how your credit history affects your ability to secure a mortgage and discuss strategies to improve or maintain a healthy credit score.

2. Budgeting for Your First Home: Buying a house is a significant financial investment, and budgeting plays a pivotal role in your ability to afford it. We'll help you create a budget that accounts for all potential expenses associated with home ownership.

3. Saving for a Down Payment and Closing Costs: Down payments and closing costs are upfront expenses that can significantly impact your ability to buy a home. We'll discuss strategies to save for these costs, including down payment assistance programs and negotiation strategies.

4. Managing Debt and Financial Responsibilities: Existing debt can affect your ability to qualify for a mortgage and manage your new home ownership responsibilities. We'll provide tips on managing and reducing debt to improve your financial readiness.

Throughout this chapter, we will share practical advice, real-life stories, and actionable steps to help you navigate the financial aspects of buying your first house. Remember that while the path to home ownership may seem daunting at times, it is a journey that, with careful planning and determination, can lead you to the doorstep of your dream home. So, let's begin the process of assessing your financial readiness and take the first step towards turning your home ownership dream into a reality.

Evaluating Your Credit Score

Your credit score is a financial fingerprint that can significantly impact your ability to secure a mortgage and the terms you'll receive. In this section, we'll delve into the importance of your credit score, how it's calculated, and steps you can take to evaluate and potentially improve it.

Understanding the Significance of Your Credit Score:

Your credit score is a three-digit number that reflects your creditworthiness. Lenders use it to assess the risk of lending you money, including when you apply for a mortgage. The higher your credit score, the more favorable terms and interest rates you can secure. Conversely, a lower score can result in higher costs or even mortgage denial.

How Credit Scores Are Calculated:

Credit scores are typically calculated using information from your credit reports, which are compiled by credit bureaus such as Equifax, Experian, and TransUnion. The most common credit scoring model is the FICO score, which ranges from 300 to 850. Here's a breakdown of the key factors that influence your credit score:

1. Payment History (35%): This is the most critical factor. It reflects whether you've paid your bills on time, including credit card payments, loans, and other debts.

2. Credit Utilization (30%): This considers the amount of credit you're currently using compared to your total available credit. Keeping your credit utilization low is crucial for a high score.

3. Length of Credit History (15%): The length of time you've had credit accounts, including the age of your oldest account, plays a role in your score.

4. Credit Mix (10%): A diverse mix of credit types, such as credit cards, installment loans, and mortgages, can positively impact your score.

5. New Credit (10%): Opening multiple new credit accounts in a short period can lower your score temporarily.

Steps to Evaluate Your Credit Score:

1. Obtain Your Credit Reports: You are entitled to one free credit report from each of the three major credit bureaus annually. Visit AnnualCreditReport.com to request your reports and review them for accuracy.

2. Check Your Credit Score: Many credit card companies now provide free access to your FICO score. Alternatively, you can use online services to check your score.

3. Review Your Credit Reports Thoroughly: Look for errors, discrepancies, or accounts you don't recognize. Dispute any inaccuracies with the credit bureaus to have them corrected.

4. Understand Your Score: Understand where your credit score stands and how it compares to the typical requirements for mortgage approval. Generally, a FICO score of 620 or higher is considered fair to good for most loans.

5. Identify Areas for Improvement: If your credit score is lower than desired, focus on the factors within your control to improve it. This may include paying bills on time, reducing outstanding debt, and avoiding new credit applications.

6. Seek Professional Help if Necessary: If you have complex credit issues or need personalized guidance, consider working with a credit counselor or financial advisor.

Your credit score is a crucial aspect of your financial readiness for home ownership. By taking the time to evaluate and, if needed, improve your credit score, you can enhance your chances of securing a mortgage with favorable terms, making your journey towards owning your first house more attainable and cost-effective.

Budgeting for Your First Home

Creating a comprehensive budget is an essential step on your path to home ownership. This chapter will guide you through the process of budgeting for your first home, helping you gain a clear understanding of your financial situation, set realistic goals, and make informed decisions about your home purchase.

The Importance of Budgeting:

Budgeting is the foundation of financial success, especially when it comes to buying a house. It allows you to:

1. Determine Affordability: A well-structured budget helps you assess how much you can comfortably afford for your monthly mortgage payment and other home ownership expenses.

2. Track Expenses: Budgeting provides insights into your spending habits, allowing you to identify areas where you can cut back and save for your down payment and future home ownership costs.

3. Plan for the Unexpected: Owning a home comes with unexpected expenses. A budget ensures you're prepared for maintenance, repairs, and other unforeseen financial challenges.

Creating Your Home Buying Budget:

1. Assess Your Current Finances: Begin by evaluating your current income, expenses, and savings. This will provide a clear picture of your financial situation.

2. Determine Your Monthly Mortgage Payment: Use online mortgage calculators to estimate your potential monthly mortgage payment based on different loan scenarios, interest rates, and down payment amounts.

3. Account for Additional Costs: Consider other home ownership expenses, such as property taxes, homeowners insurance, and private mortgage insurance (if applicable).

4. Factor in Utilities and Maintenance: Don't forget to include ongoing costs like utilities, maintenance, and repair expenses. These can vary based on the size and condition of your home.

5. Create a Savings Plan: Develop a savings plan to cover your down payment and closing costs. Determine how much you can save each month to reach your home ownership goals.

6. Set Aside an Emergency Fund: Maintain an emergency fund for unexpected expenses. Financial experts often recommend saving three to six months' worth of living expenses.

7. Review and Adjust Regularly: Your budget isn't set in stone. Periodically review and adjust it to reflect changes in your financial situation or housing market conditions.

Budgeting Tips for Homebuyers:

- Prioritize Savings: Make saving for your down payment and closing costs a top priority in your budget. Consider opening a separate savings account dedicated to your home purchase.

- Cut Unnecessary Expenses: Identify discretionary spending and consider cutting back to increase your savings. This may involve dining out less, canceling unused subscriptions, or reducing impulse purchases.

- Avoid Taking on New Debt: Minimize new debt, such as credit card balances or personal loans, as it can affect your ability to qualify for a mortgage.

- Seek Professional Guidance: If you're struggling to create an effective budget, consider working with a financial advisor or housing counselor who specializes in home ownership.

Creating and sticking to a budget may require discipline and sacrifice, but it is a critical step in achieving your dream of owning your first home. A well-managed budget not only helps you determine what you can afford but also provides financial stability and peace of mind as you embark on this exciting journey towards home ownership.

Saving for a Down Payment and Closing Costs

Saving for a down payment and covering closing costs are two of the most significant financial hurdles you'll encounter when buying your first home. This chapter is your guide to understanding these costs, creating a savings plan, and taking steps to accumulate the funds needed to make your home ownership dream a reality.

Understanding Down Payments and Closing Costs:

1. Down Payment: The down payment is a substantial upfront payment you make towards the purchase price of your home. It's typically expressed as a percentage of the total home price. The amount required varies but is often around 20% of the home's purchase price. However, some loan programs offer lower down payment options.

2. Closing Costs: Closing costs are the various fees and expenses associated with finalizing the purchase of your home. These costs can include loan origination fees, appraisal fees, title insurance, attorney fees, and more. Closing costs typically range from 2% to 5% of the home's purchase price.

Creating a Savings Plan:

1. Set Clear Savings Goals: Determine how much you need for a down payment and closing costs based on your target home price and the percentage required in your area. Be sure to consider additional costs for moving, initial home improvements, and an emergency fund.

2. Establish a Separate Savings Account: Open a dedicated savings account for your down payment and closing costs. This will help you keep the funds separate from your everyday spending money.

3. Automate Your Savings: Set up automatic transfers from your checking account to your savings account on a regular basis. Treating your savings like a non-negotiable expense ensures consistent progress.

4. Cut Discretionary Expenses: Review your monthly spending habits and identify areas where you can cut back. Redirect the money saved towards your down payment fund.

5. Increase Your Income: Consider ways to boost your income, such as taking on a part-time job, freelancing, or selling unused items. Every extra dollar can make a difference.

6. Leverage Windfalls: Put any unexpected windfalls, such as tax refunds, work bonuses, or gifts, directly into your down payment savings account.

Exploring Down Payment Assistance:

1. Government Programs: Investigate government-backed programs that offer down payment assistance, especially if you're a first-time homebuyer or have a lower income. These programs vary by location and may provide grants, loans, or tax incentives.

2. Employer Benefits: Check if your employer offers home buying assistance programs or employer-assisted housing initiatives.

3. Gifts and Family Support: Some homebuyers receive financial assistance from family members or friends. Be aware that lenders may have specific rules about gift funds, so consult with your lender.

Planning for Closing Costs:

1. Request Closing Cost Estimates: During the homebuying process, ask your lender for a Good Faith Estimate (GFE) or a Loan Estimate (LE). These documents outline your expected closing costs, helping you budget accordingly.

2. Negotiate with the Seller: In some cases, you may negotiate with the seller to cover a portion of the closing costs as part of the purchase agreement.

Monitor Your Progress:

Regularly review your savings plan and adjust it as needed. Keep a close eye on your credit score, as a higher score can lead to better mortgage terms, potentially reducing your upfront costs. As you inch closer to your savings goals, stay motivated by visualizing the moment when you hand over the keys to your new home. Saving for a down payment and closing costs requires patience and discipline, but with a well-executed plan, you'll be one step closer to home ownership.

Managing Debt and Financial Responsibilities

When preparing to buy your first home, managing your debt and financial responsibilities is essential. Lenders closely examine your financial stability and debt-to-income ratio to determine your eligibility for a mortgage. In this chapter, we'll explore strategies to effectively manage debt, improve your financial standing, and ensure you're well-positioned to secure a mortgage for your dream home.

Understanding Debt and Its Impact:

1. Types of Debt: Debt comes in various forms, such as credit card debt, student loans, car loans, and personal loans. Each type can impact your credit score and overall financial health differently.

2. Debt-to-Income Ratio (DTI): Lenders assess your DTI to determine how much of your monthly income goes toward paying debt. A high DTI can make it challenging to qualify for a mortgage.

Strategies for Managing Debt:

1. Create a Debt Inventory: List all your debts, including outstanding balances, interest rates, and minimum monthly payments. This inventory provides a clear picture of your financial obligations.

2. Prioritize High-Interest Debt: Focus on paying off high-interest debts first, as they cost you more

over time. Consider strategies like the debt snowball or debt avalanche method to tackle multiple debts.

3. Consolidate or Refinance: Explore options to consolidate or refinance high-interest loans to lower your monthly payments and reduce interest costs.

4. Avoid New Debt: While saving for your home, minimize new debt and avoid making large purchases on credit that could negatively affect your credit score and DTI.

5. Pay Bills on Time: Consistently paying bills on time is crucial for maintaining or improving your credit score. Consider setting up automatic payments to avoid missed deadlines.

6. Negotiate Lower Interest Rates: Contact your creditors to negotiate lower interest rates, especially if you have a history of on-time payments.

Improving Your Financial Standing:

1. Emergency Fund: Build and maintain an emergency fund with at least three to six months' worth of living expenses. This fund serves as a safety net during unexpected financial challenges.

2. Increase Your Income: Seek opportunities to increase your income through side gigs, freelancing, or seeking a higher-paying job.

3. Create a Realistic Budget: Develop a budget that includes your debt payments, savings goals, and living expenses. Stick to it to maintain financial discipline.

4. Boost Your Credit Score: Regularly monitor your credit score and take steps to improve it, such as reducing credit card balances and disputing inaccuracies on your credit report.

Working with a Housing Counselor:

Consider seeking guidance from a HUD-approved housing counselor or financial advisor who specializes in home ownership. They can provide personalized advice on managing your finances and preparing for home ownership.

By effectively managing your debt and financial responsibilities, you not only improve your chances of securing a mortgage but also set yourself up for a successful and sustainable home ownership journey. Remember that financial stability and responsible debt management are key factors in achieving your goal of owning your first home.

Chapter 2: Finding the Right Real Estate Agent

The process of buying your first home can be both thrilling and overwhelming, filled with choices that will shape your journey towards home ownership. One of the most significant decisions you'll make is choosing the right real estate agent to guide you through this adventure. In this chapter, we'll explore the pivotal role of a real estate agent, how to select the right one for your needs, and the importance of building a trusting partnership.

The Real Estate Agent: Your Guide and Advocate

A real estate agent is more than just a professional who helps you find properties; they are your advocate, confidant, and expert advisor on all things related to buying a home. Their expertise, local knowledge, and negotiation skills are invaluable assets as you navigate the real estate market.

In the pages that follow, we'll take a deep dive into the process of finding the perfect real estate agent who will be your partner throughout this journey. We'll discuss the various roles they play, the qualities to look for, and the questions to ask during the selection process. Whether you're a first-time buyer or seeking a better fit for your specific needs, this chapter will equip you with the knowledge and confidence to make an informed choice.

Remember that your real estate agent is not just a professional hired to find you a house; they are your ally in achieving the dream of home ownership. So, let's embark on the exploration of finding the right real estate agent to make this dream a reality.

The Role of a Real Estate Agent

When it comes to buying your first home, a real estate agent is your invaluable guide and partner throughout the entire journey. Understanding the multifaceted role they play can help you appreciate the significance of selecting the right agent for your needs. In this section, we'll explore the essential roles that real estate agents fulfill in the home-buying process:

1. Market Expertise: Real estate agents are intimately familiar with the local housing market. They can provide insights into neighborhood trends, property values, and potential growth areas, helping you make informed decisions.

2. Property Search: Your agent will assist in narrowing down your property search based on your preferences, budget, and desired features. They have access to listings that may not be readily available to the public.

3. Property Evaluation: Agents help you assess properties, pointing out both strengths and weaknesses. They consider factors like condition, resale value, and potential for appreciation.

4. Negotiation: One of the most critical roles of a real estate agent is negotiating on your behalf. They aim to secure the best possible terms for your purchase, from the initial offer to counteroffers, inspections, and repairs.

5. Paperwork and Documentation: The home-buying process involves a significant amount of paperwork. Your agent will ensure that all documents are properly completed and submitted, avoiding potential legal issues.

6. Connections: Agents have an extensive network of professionals, including mortgage brokers, inspectors, attorneys, and contractors. They can recommend trusted professionals to assist you throughout the process.

7. Problem-Solving: Challenges can arise during a home purchase, from financing issues to unexpected repairs. Your agent's experience and problem-solving skills are invaluable in overcoming these obstacles.

8. Advice and Guidance: Your agent will provide guidance on making competitive offers, navigating

contingencies, and addressing concerns throughout the transaction.

9. Closing Coordination: Leading up to closing day, your agent will work with all parties involved, including the seller's agent, lender, and title company, to ensure a smooth and successful closing.

10. Post-Purchase Support: Even after closing, your agent can be a valuable resource, providing recommendations for home maintenance, local services, and any questions or concerns that may arise as you settle into your new home.

The Importance of a Trusting Relationship:

The relationship you build with your real estate agent is crucial to the success of your home purchase. Open communication, trust, and a shared vision are essential elements of a strong partnership. Your agent should prioritize your interests and work tirelessly to help you achieve your home ownership goals.

As you embark on the process of selecting a real estate agent, keep in mind that you're not just choosing a professional; you're selecting a trusted partner who will be by your side, offering guidance and support as you navigate the complexities of the real estate market. Choosing the right agent is a critical decision that can greatly influence the outcome of your home-buying journey.

How to Choose the Right Agent for You

Selecting the right real estate agent is a crucial step in your journey to home ownership. The agent you choose will play a pivotal role in helping you find your dream home, negotiate favorable terms, and navigate the complexities of the real estate market. Here are essential steps and considerations to guide you in choosing the perfect agent for your needs:

1. Define Your Needs and Preferences:
   - Clarify your priorities. What type of property are you looking for? What are your must-haves and deal-breakers?
   - Consider your communication preferences. Do you prefer phone calls, emails, or in-person meetings?
   - Think about your timeline. How quickly do you need to find and purchase a home?

2. Seek Recommendations:
   - Ask friends, family, and colleagues for referrals. Personal recommendations can provide valuable insights into an agent's professionalism and service.
   - Read online reviews and testimonials to get a sense of an agent's reputation and track record.

3. Research Local Agents:
   - Identify real estate agents who specialize in the area where you want to buy a home. Local expertise is essential for finding the right property.
   - Check licensing and credentials. Ensure the agent is licensed and in good standing with relevant local real estate authorities.

4. Interview Multiple Agents:
   - Don't hesitate to interview multiple agents to find the best fit. Ask questions about their experience, recent transactions, and their approach to helping buyers.

- Inquire about their availability and responsiveness. Ensure they can accommodate your schedule and communication preferences.

5. Assess Compatibility:
  - Consider the agent's personality and communication style. You'll be working closely with them, so a good rapport is crucial.
  - Gauge their willingness to listen and understand your unique needs and preferences.

6. Check References:
  - Request references from past clients and contact them to learn about their experiences working with the agent.
  - Ask about the agent's negotiation skills, problem-solving abilities, and overall professionalism.

7. Evaluate Market Knowledge:
  - Assess the agent's knowledge of the local real estate market. They should be able to provide insights into current trends, pricing, and neighborhoods.
  - Inquire about their access to market data and tools for property searches.

8. Review the Agent's Track Record:
  - Look into the agent's recent sales and transactions. A successful track record suggests competence and experience.
  - Check if they have experience with first-time homebuyers or specific property types you're interested in.

9. Discuss Fees and Contracts:
  - Have a transparent discussion about the agent's fees and commissions. Ensure you understand the terms of your agreement before moving forward.
  - Be wary of agents who pressure you to sign exclusive contracts without thoroughly explaining the terms.

10. Trust Your Instincts:
  - Ultimately, trust your instincts when choosing an agent. If you feel comfortable and confident in their abilities, it's a positive sign.

Selecting the right real estate agent is a crucial step towards a successful homebuying experience. Take your time to assess your needs, research agents, and interview candidates. By following these steps and considering your preferences and priorities, you can find the agent who will guide you through the process and help you achieve your home ownership goals.

Interviewing Potential Agents

Once you've compiled a list of potential real estate agents, the next step is to interview them to find the one who aligns best with your needs and preferences. This process will help you gain insight into their qualifications, experience, and approach to helping you find your dream home. Here's a comprehensive guide on how to conduct effective interviews with potential real estate agents:

1. Schedule Initial Meetings:
  - Reach out to the agents you're interested in and schedule initial meetings. These meetings can be conducted in person or virtually, depending on your preference.

2. Prepare a List of Questions:
   - Before the meeting, prepare a list of questions to ask each agent. This will help you compare their responses and assess their suitability for your needs.

3. Assess Experience and Expertise:
   - Inquire about their experience as a real estate agent, especially their experience in the local market. Ask how long they've been in the industry and their track record with similar transactions.

4. Ask About Their Approach:
   - Understand their approach to helping buyers. Ask about their strategy for finding properties that match your criteria and their negotiation tactics.

5. Discuss Market Knowledge:
   - Assess their knowledge of the local real estate market. They should be able to provide insights into neighborhood trends, pricing, and the current state of the market.

6. Evaluate Communication and Availability:
   - Discuss their availability and communication style. Ask how they prefer to communicate and how quickly they typically respond to client inquiries.

7. Inquire About Their Network:
   - Ask about their professional network, including connections with lenders, inspectors, contractors, and other professionals you may need during the home-buying process.

8. Request References:
   - Request references from past clients. Contact these references to gain firsthand insight into their experiences working with the agent.

9. Discuss Compensation:
   - Have a transparent conversation about the agent's fees and commissions. Ensure you understand how their compensation structure works.

10. Evaluate Compatibility:
    - Assess the agent's personality and interpersonal skills. A good working relationship is essential, so consider whether you feel comfortable and confident in their abilities.

11. Review Marketing and Technology Tools:
    - If applicable, discuss the agent's marketing and technology tools. This can include their use of online listings, virtual tours, or other resources to help you find properties.

12. Ask About Handling Contingencies:
    - Discuss how the agent handles contingencies in offers, such as home inspections, appraisals, and financing. Their expertise in managing these aspects can be critical.

13. Clarify Contract Terms:
    - If you decide to move forward with an agent, ensure you fully understand the terms of the agreement, including the duration and exclusivity, if any.

14. Trust Your Instincts:
   - Pay attention to your gut feeling during the interview. Trust your instincts when assessing whether the agent is the right fit for you.

15. Compare Responses:
   - After interviewing multiple agents, compare their responses, qualifications, and overall impressions. Consider who best aligns with your goals and preferences.

By conducting thorough interviews with potential real estate agents, you'll be well-equipped to make an informed decision. Remember that this is a significant partnership, and selecting the right agent can greatly impact your home-buying experience. Take your time to find the agent who will help you navigate the path to home ownership successfully.

Building a Trusting Relationship

In the world of real estate, trust is the cornerstone of a successful partnership between you and your real estate agent. As you progress in your journey to home ownership, nurturing a trusting relationship with your agent is essential. This chapter explores the vital elements of building and maintaining trust throughout the home-buying process.

Why Trust Matters:

Trust is the foundation of a strong working relationship with your real estate agent. Here's why it's paramount:

1. Open Communication: Trust encourages open and honest communication, enabling you to express your needs, concerns, and preferences freely.

2. Confidence in Decision-Making: When you trust your agent's expertise and advice, you can make confident and well-informed decisions about your home purchase.

3. Efficiency and Collaboration: Trust fosters efficient collaboration. You and your agent can work seamlessly together towards your home ownership goals.

4. Negotiation and Advocacy: A trusting relationship empowers your agent to negotiate on your behalf and advocate for your interests effectively.

Elements of a Trusting Relationship:

1. Transparency: Be transparent with your agent about your budget, preferences, and any concerns you may have. Honesty is key to a successful partnership.

2. Active Listening: Your agent should actively listen to your needs and priorities. Similarly, listen to their insights and advice.

3. Respect: Treat your agent with respect, and expect the same in return. Respectful communication forms the basis of trust.

4. Professionalism: Expect professionalism from your agent. They should be punctual, responsive, and

knowledgeable about the market.

5. Timely Communication: Keep communication lines open and timely. If you have questions or concerns, don't hesitate to reach out to your agent.

6. Collaboration: Work collaboratively with your agent. Understand that their role is to guide and assist you, but your input and decisions are crucial.

The Agent's Role in Building Trust:

Your real estate agent plays a significant role in fostering trust. Look for these qualities and actions in your agent:

1. Transparency: Your agent should be upfront about any potential conflicts of interest, property issues, or market conditions that may impact your decision-making.

2. Expertise: Trust in your agent's expertise. They should provide market insights, property information, and guidance based on their knowledge and experience.

3. Availability: Your agent should be accessible and responsive to your inquiries and needs. A lack of responsiveness can erode trust.

4. Consistent Communication: Your agent should keep you informed about the progress of your home search, negotiations, and transaction details.

5. Negotiation Skills: Trust your agent's negotiation skills to secure the best terms for your purchase.

6. Ethical Conduct: Ensure your agent adheres to ethical standards and follows industry regulations.

Maintaining Trust:

Building trust is an ongoing process. Here's how to maintain trust throughout your home-buying journey:

1. Regular Updates: Stay informed about the progress of your transaction with regular updates from your agent.

2. Ask Questions: Don't hesitate to ask questions or seek clarification when needed. Open dialogue reinforces trust.

3. Express Concerns: If you have concerns, share them with your agent. Addressing issues promptly can strengthen trust.

4. Feedback: Provide feedback to your agent about your experiences and interactions. This can help improve the partnership.

5. Trust the Process: Trust that your agent is working in your best interests. Avoid micromanaging or second-guessing their actions.

Building and maintaining a trusting relationship with your real estate agent is a fundamental aspect of a successful home-buying journey. By prioritizing open communication, respect, and professionalism, you can ensure a partnership built on trust that will guide you toward the realization of your home ownership dream.

Chapter 3: Navigating the Real Estate Market

As you embark on your journey to become a homeowner, you'll find yourself navigating the dynamic and ever-changing world of the real estate market. Chapter 3 is your compass, helping you understand the complexities of this market, from identifying trends to evaluating property values and negotiating offers. This chapter is designed to empower you with the knowledge and strategies you need to make informed decisions in the fast-paced world of real estate.

The Real Estate Market: A Shifting Landscape

The real estate market is not a static entity but a dynamic ecosystem influenced by a multitude of factors – economic conditions, interest rates, local trends, and even seasons. Understanding these variables is essential as they will shape your home-buying experience. In this chapter, we'll explore how to navigate this intricate landscape and adapt to changing conditions while staying focused on your home ownership goals.

What Awaits You:

1. Evaluating Market Conditions: We'll delve into the importance of understanding whether you're in a buyer's market, seller's market, or a balanced market. This knowledge will guide your negotiation strategies and timing.

2. Property Values and Pricing: Learn how to assess property values and price trends in your desired neighborhood. Discover the tools and resources available to help you make informed decisions about property affordability.

3. The Art of Property Search: Master the art of property search, from online listings and real estate apps to open houses and working with your real estate agent. You'll gain insights into efficient search techniques.

4. Analyzing Property Listings: We'll dissect property listings, helping you decode descriptions, photos, and listing details to identify potential gems and red flags.

5. Property Inspections and Due Diligence: Understand the importance of property inspections and conducting due diligence to ensure that the home you choose meets your expectations and is in good condition.

6. The Offer and Negotiation Process: Learn how to prepare and submit a compelling offer. We'll also explore negotiation strategies to help you secure favorable terms in competitive markets.

7. Contract and Closing: Once your offer is accepted, we'll guide you through the contract and closing process, including inspections, appraisals, and final preparations for home ownership.

Empower Yourself in the Real Estate Market:

Navigating the real estate market can be both exciting and challenging. By the end of this chapter, you'll be equipped with the knowledge and tools to navigate the market confidently, make informed decisions, and pursue your dream of home ownership with clarity and purpose. The real estate market may be dynamic, but with the right guidance and understanding, you can navigate its twists and turns successfully.

Types of Properties

The real estate market offers a diverse range of properties to suit various lifestyles, preferences, and budgets. As you navigate your journey to home ownership, it's essential to familiarize yourself with the different types of properties available. Understanding these options will help you narrow down your search and find the perfect home that aligns with your needs and desires. Here are some common types of properties you may encounter:

1. Single-Family Homes:
   - Description: Single-family homes are standalone structures designed to accommodate one family. They typically have their own yard and are not attached to other dwellings.
   - Advantages: Privacy, outdoor space, and potential for future expansion or customization.
   - Considerations: Maintenance responsibilities and potentially higher costs compared to other property types.

2. Condominiums (Condos):
   - Description: Condos are individual units within a larger building or complex. Owners have ownership of their unit but share common areas and maintenance costs with other residents.
   - Advantages: Lower maintenance, amenities (e.g., pool, gym), and potentially lower purchase prices in some areas.
   - Considerations: Monthly homeowners' association (HOA) fees, shared decision-making, and limited control over common areas.

3. Townhouses:
   - Description: Townhouses are multi-level homes attached to other units in a row or a block. They combine elements of single-family homes and condos.
   - Advantages: Generally more affordable than single-family homes, often include shared amenities, and require less maintenance than detached houses.
   - Considerations: HOA fees, shared walls (potential noise), and limited outdoor space.

4. Multi-Family Homes:
   - Description: Multi-family properties consist of multiple separate living units within the same structure. Examples include duplexes, triplexes, and apartment buildings.
   - Advantages: Rental income potential, shared expenses, and investment opportunities.
   - Considerations: Landlord responsibilities, property management, and potential for vacancies.

5. Co-ops (Cooperative Apartments):
   - Description: Co-ops are a unique form of home ownership where residents own shares in a corporation that owns the building. Each resident has a proprietary lease on their unit.
   - Advantages: Potential for lower purchase prices, community-oriented, and shared expenses.
   - Considerations: Strict board approval process, limited control over changes to your unit, and monthly maintenance fees.

6. Mobile Homes:
   - Description: Mobile homes are factory-built dwellings that can be placed on leased land or in mobile home parks.
   - Advantages: Affordability, mobility (can be relocated), and often lower property taxes.
   - Considerations: Lease or park fees, potential depreciation, and limited appreciation compared to traditional homes.

7. Vacation Homes:
   - Description: Vacation homes are properties purchased primarily for recreational purposes. They can be single-family homes, condos, or cabins located in desirable vacation destinations.
   - Advantages: Personal use for vacations, potential rental income, and long-term investment.
   - Considerations: Seasonal demand, maintenance from a distance, and property management for rentals.

8. New Construction:
   - Description: New construction properties are homes or condos built from the ground up. Buyers can often customize features and finishes.
   - Advantages: Modern amenities, energy efficiency, and the opportunity to personalize your home.
   - Considerations: Potentially higher costs, construction timelines, and the need to make decisions on design and features.

9. Historic Homes:
   - Description: Historic homes are properties with architectural or historical significance. They may be protected by preservation laws.
   - Advantages: Unique character, potential tax incentives for restoration, and a connection to history.
   - Considerations: Maintenance challenges, potential restrictions on renovations, and higher costs for restoration.

Each type of property comes with its own set of advantages and considerations. Your choice will depend on your lifestyle, financial situation, and personal preferences. As you explore the real estate market, take the time to weigh these factors and find the property type that best aligns with your vision of home ownership.

Understanding Market Trends

In the ever-evolving world of real estate, market trends play a significant role in shaping your home-buying experience. Being aware of these trends and understanding their implications can empower you to make informed decisions and navigate the real estate market more effectively. In this section, we'll delve into the importance of understanding market trends and explore key factors that influence them:

Why Market Trends Matter:

1. Informed Decision-Making: Understanding current market trends helps you make informed decisions about when and where to buy a home.

2. Price Expectations: It allows you to set realistic expectations regarding property prices and potential appreciation or depreciation.

3. Competitive Advantage: Being aware of trends gives you a competitive advantage when negotiating offers, especially in a competitive market.

4. Financial Planning: Market trends influence interest rates, which can impact your mortgage financing. Knowing these trends can help you plan your budget.

Key Factors Influencing Market Trends:

1. Economic Conditions: The overall economic health of the country, including factors like employment rates, inflation, and GDP growth, can influence the real estate market.

2. Interest Rates: Mortgage interest rates significantly affect the real estate market. Lower rates generally stimulate demand, while higher rates can slow it down.

3. Supply and Demand: The balance between the number of available properties (supply) and the number of buyers (demand) in a particular area influences pricing and market conditions.

4. Location: Real estate is inherently local. Market trends can vary from one neighborhood or city to another, so location is a critical factor.

5. Demographics: Population trends, such as age, migration patterns, and household composition, can impact housing demand.

6. Government Policies: Government policies, including tax incentives, zoning regulations, and lending practices, can have a significant impact on the real estate market.

Types of Market Trends:

1. Seller's Market: In a seller's market, demand for homes exceeds supply, leading to rising prices and competitive bidding among buyers.

2. Buyer's Market: A buyer's market occurs when there are more homes available than buyers, leading to lower prices and more favorable terms for buyers.

3. Balanced Market: A balanced market strikes a healthy equilibrium between supply and demand, resulting in stable prices and reasonable negotiation conditions for both buyers and sellers.

4. Seasonal Trends: Real estate markets often exhibit seasonal fluctuations, with spring and summer typically being more active for home sales.

5. Long-Term Appreciation: Over the long term, real estate tends to appreciate in value, making it an attractive investment.

Staying Informed:

To stay informed about market trends, consider these strategies:

1. Consult Your Real Estate Agent: Your agent can provide insights into local market conditions and recent sales data.

2. Research Online: Utilize online resources, such as real estate websites and market reports, to track trends in your desired area.

3. Attend Open Houses: Visiting open houses can give you a firsthand look at current market conditions and property values.

4. Talk to Local Experts: Engage with local real estate experts, economists, or appraisers who have an in-depth understanding of your market.

5. Follow News and Economic Reports: Stay updated on economic news and reports that may impact the housing market.

Understanding market trends is a valuable skill for any homebuyer. By staying informed and considering the factors that influence these trends, you'll be better equipped to make sound decisions throughout your home ownership journey. Whether you're buying in a seller's, buyer's, or balanced market, your knowledge of market trends will help you navigate the real estate landscape with confidence.

Determining Your Preferred Location

Choosing the right location for your future home is a crucial aspect of the home-buying process. The location you select will significantly impact your lifestyle, daily commute, access to amenities, and overall satisfaction with your new home. In this section, we'll guide you through the process of determining your preferred location by considering various factors:

1. Commute and Accessibility:
   - Consider your daily commute to work, school, or other frequently visited places. Determine your tolerance for commute times and traffic conditions.
   - Explore the accessibility of the location in terms of public transportation, highways, and proximity to major roads.

2. Neighborhood and Community:
   - Assess the neighborhood's character and ambiance. Are you looking for a quiet suburban area, a bustling urban neighborhood, or a peaceful rural setting?
   - Research the community's amenities, such as parks, schools, healthcare facilities, shopping centers, and recreational options.

3. Safety and Security:
   - Investigate the safety and crime rates in the area. You can access crime statistics from local law enforcement agencies or online databases.
   - Consult with local residents or neighborhood associations to get insights into the area's safety.

4. Schools and Education:
   - If you have children or plan to in the future, research the quality of local schools, both public and private.
   - Consider the proximity of educational institutions and their reputation.

5. Lifestyle and Recreation:

- Think about your lifestyle preferences. Are you interested in cultural events, dining, outdoor activities, or nightlife? Ensure the location aligns with your interests.
   - Research nearby recreational facilities, such as gyms, sports clubs, and cultural venues.

6. Cost of Living:
   - Evaluate the cost of living in the area, including property taxes, utility costs, and local services.
   - Compare the cost of living to your budget and financial goals.

7. Future Development:
   - Investigate any planned or ongoing development projects in the area. This can affect property values and your long-term investment.
   - Consider the potential impact of future development on traffic and the neighborhood's character.

8. Resale Value:
   - Think about the potential resale value of the property. Locations with strong demand and desirable features often appreciate more over time.

9. Noise and Environmental Factors:
   - Pay attention to noise levels and environmental factors in the area, such as proximity to highways, airports, or industrial zones.
   - Visit the neighborhood at different times of the day to gauge noise levels.

10. Personal Preferences:
    - Reflect on your personal preferences, including proximity to family and friends, favorite places, and the overall "feel" of the location.

Prioritizing Your Criteria:

Once you've considered these factors, prioritize your criteria based on their importance to you and your family. It's unlikely that any location will meet every criterion perfectly, so identifying your top priorities will help you make a more focused decision.

Consult with a Local Real Estate Agent:

A local real estate agent with expertise in the area can be an invaluable resource. They can provide insights into neighborhoods, market conditions, and available properties that align with your preferences.

Exploring Potential Locations:

Take the time to explore potential locations by visiting neighborhoods, attending open houses, and interacting with local residents. This firsthand experience will help you get a feel for each area and make an informed choice.

Choosing the right location is a significant step towards finding your ideal home. By carefully considering these factors and prioritizing your criteria, you can identify the location that best suits your lifestyle and aligns with your long-term goals for home ownership.

Online and Offline Property Searches

In your quest to find the perfect home, you have at your disposal a plethora of resources for property searches, both online and offline. These methods offer different advantages and can be used individually or in combination to maximize your chances of finding the ideal property. Let's explore both online and offline property search options:

Online Property Searches:

1. Real Estate Websites: Online platforms such as Zillow, Realtor.com, Trulia, and Redfin provide extensive listings of properties for sale. These websites allow you to filter your search by location, price range, property type, and specific features.

2. Mobile Apps: Many real estate websites offer mobile apps for convenient property searches on smartphones and tablets. These apps often include features like GPS-based property search and saved searches.

3. Social Media: Real estate agents and agencies frequently post property listings on social media platforms like Facebook, Instagram, and Twitter. Following local real estate pages can help you discover new listings.

4. Virtual Tours: Some listings offer virtual tours, 3D walkthroughs, or video presentations, allowing you to explore properties from the comfort of your home before scheduling an in-person visit.

5. Email Alerts: Sign up for email alerts on real estate websites to receive notifications when properties that match your criteria become available.

6. Online Forums and Groups: Participate in online forums or social media groups related to real estate in your desired location. Members often share information about listings and market trends.

Offline Property Searches:

1. Real Estate Agents: Local real estate agents have access to listings not always available online. They can provide personalized assistance, schedule property showings, and offer insights into the local market.

2. Open Houses: Attend open houses in your target area. This allows you to explore properties, meet real estate agents, and get a feel for the neighborhood.

3. Real Estate Magazines: Many regions have real estate magazines or newspapers that feature property listings. These publications are available at supermarkets, libraries, and real estate offices.

4. Networking: Talk to friends, family, and colleagues about your home-buying plans. They may know someone selling a property or recommend a reputable real estate agent.

5. Local Government Offices: Visit local government offices or municipal websites to inquire about property listings, tax records, and zoning regulations.

6. Drive or Walk Around: Explore your desired neighborhoods by driving or walking around. You may discover "For Sale" signs or properties not yet listed online.

7. Community Bulletin Boards: Check community bulletin boards at local businesses, community centers, or places of worship for property listings and real estate services.

Combining Online and Offline Searches:

To maximize your property search efforts, consider combining online and offline methods. Online resources provide a broad view of available properties, while offline methods offer a more personal touch and access to unadvertised listings.

Remember to stay organized throughout your search by keeping notes, photos, and details of the properties you explore. Collaborate closely with your real estate agent, whether you find them online or through offline referrals, to streamline the process and find your dream home efficiently.

Chapter 4: Getting Pre-Approved for a Mortgage

Securing a mortgage is a pivotal step in the home-buying journey. It's the financial cornerstone upon which your home ownership dreams will be built. But before you start browsing properties or making offers, there's a crucial step that can save you time, prevent disappointment, and give you a clear picture of your purchasing power: getting pre-approved for a mortgage.

The Importance of Mortgage Pre-Approval:

Mortgage pre-approval is more than just a formality; it's a strategic move that can give you an edge in a competitive real estate market. In this chapter, we'll delve into the significance of mortgage pre-approval and how it empowers you as a homebuyer:

A Competitive Advantage: Discover how pre-approval makes your offers more attractive to sellers, as they know you're a serious and qualified buyer.

Budget Clarity: Gain a comprehensive understanding of your budget and the price range within which you should be searching for homes.

Negotiating Power: Learn how pre-approval enhances your negotiation position, allowing you to act swiftly and confidently when you find the right property.

Avoiding Disappointment: Prevent the heartbreak of falling in love with a home that's out of your financial reach by determining your budget upfront.

The Pre-Approval Process:

We'll guide you through the steps of the pre-approval process, helping you understand what lenders evaluate when considering your application. From creditworthiness and income verification to debt ratios and down payment requirements, we'll break down the criteria that lenders assess to determine your eligibility for a mortgage.

Choosing the Right Lender:

Selecting the right lender is a crucial decision. We'll provide insights into factors to consider when choosing a lender, including interest rates, loan types, and customer service.

Preparing for Success:

Prepare yourself for a successful pre-approval process by gathering necessary documentation, understanding credit reports, and addressing any potential hurdles that may arise.

Your Mortgage Pre-Approval Journey Begins Here:

Mortgage pre-approval is the key that unlocks the doors to home ownership. As you embark on this chapter, you're taking a significant step towards securing the financial foundation needed to turn your home ownership dreams into reality. Whether you're a first-time buyer or a seasoned homeowner, understanding the mortgage pre-approval process is essential to making informed decisions and navigating the real estate market with confidence. Let's dive into the world of mortgage pre-approval and pave the way to your new home.

The Importance of Mortgage Pre-Approval

Mortgage pre-approval is not just a preliminary step in the home-buying process; it's a powerful tool that can make a significant difference in your real estate journey. Here, we'll explore the importance of mortgage pre-approval and why it should be a fundamental part of your homebuying strategy.

1. A Competitive Advantage:
   - In a competitive real estate market, where multiple buyers may be interested in the same property, pre-approval sets you apart as a serious and qualified buyer. Sellers often prioritize offers from pre-approved buyers, as they are more likely to secure financing.

2. Budget Clarity:
   - Pre-approval provides a clear understanding of your budget. By assessing your financial situation, a lender determines the maximum mortgage amount you can borrow. This information helps you focus your property search on homes within your price range.

3. Negotiating Power:
   - When you're pre-approved, you have the upper hand in negotiations. Sellers are more inclined to negotiate with buyers who have their financing in order, which can lead to better terms and potentially a lower purchase price.

4. Avoiding Disappointment:
   - There's nothing more disheartening than falling in love with a home only to discover it's beyond your financial reach. Pre-approval prevents such disappointment by ensuring you look at homes that match your budget.

5. Faster Closing Process:
   - A pre-approved buyer can often expedite the closing process, as much of the required documentation and credit checks have already been completed. This can be appealing to both sellers and real estate professionals.

6. Confidence in Offers:
   - With pre-approval, you can confidently make offers on properties you're interested in, knowing that

you have the financial backing to proceed. This assertiveness can be particularly valuable in competitive markets.

7. Identification of Potential Issues:
   - During the pre-approval process, potential issues with your credit or financial history may arise. Identifying these problems early allows you to address them and improve your eligibility for a mortgage.

8. Customized Financing Options:
   - Pre-approval enables you to explore various mortgage options and choose the one that best suits your needs and financial goals. You can compare interest rates, terms, and down payment requirements.

9. Realistic Expectations:
   - With pre-approval, you have a realistic perspective on what you can afford. This helps you set reasonable expectations for your home search and avoids wasting time on properties that don't align with your budget.

10. Smooth Homebuying Experience:
    - A pre-approval sets the stage for a smoother and more efficient homebuying process. It streamlines the transaction and minimizes surprises along the way.

In summary, mortgage pre-approval is a valuable tool that not only enhances your position as a buyer but also provides clarity, confidence, and a competitive edge. It's a proactive step that demonstrates your commitment to the home-buying process and ensures you're well-prepared to make one of the most significant financial decisions of your life. So, before you embark on your homebuying journey, consider the importance of mortgage pre-approval as a critical and empowering first step.

Preparing Your Financial Documents

As you embark on the journey of getting pre-approved for a mortgage, one of the crucial steps is gathering and preparing your financial documents. Lenders will use these documents to assess your financial stability, creditworthiness, and eligibility for a mortgage. Being well-prepared with the necessary paperwork will streamline the pre-approval process and increase your chances of securing the loan you need. Here's a comprehensive list of financial documents you should gather and prepare:

1. Proof of Identity:
   - Valid government-issued photo ID, such as a driver's license or passport.

2. Income Verification:
   - W-2 forms for the past two years if you're a salaried employee.
   - If you're self-employed or receive additional income sources, provide complete tax returns (usually for the past two years) along with all schedules, including Schedule C or E.
   - Recent pay stubs or earning statements covering the most recent 30 days.

3. Proof of Assets:
   - Bank statements for all checking, savings, and investment accounts for the past two to three months.
   - Statements for retirement accounts (e.g., 401(k), IRA).
   - Documentation for any other assets, such as stocks, bonds, or real estate properties.

4. Employment Verification:
   - A verification of employment (VOE) form signed by your employer, confirming your job position, income, and length of employment.

5. Proof of Down Payment and Closing Costs:
   - Statements showing the source of your down payment and closing costs, such as savings accounts, gifts from family members, or proceeds from the sale of assets.

6. Credit Report:
   - Lenders will obtain your credit report, but it's essential to review it yourself for any errors or discrepancies.

7. Debt Obligations:
   - A list of all your current debts, including credit cards, student loans, auto loans, and any other outstanding loans.
   - Statements for outstanding loans, including the current balance, minimum monthly payments, and terms.

8. Proof of Residence:
   - If you're renting, provide your landlord's contact information.
   - If you currently own a home, provide the mortgage statement.

9. Additional Documents:
   - Any documents related to bankruptcy, foreclosure, or short sales, if applicable.
   - Divorce decrees or separation agreements, if they impact your financial situation.
   - Proof of child support or alimony income, if applicable.
   - Rental history, if you have been renting.

10. Gift Letters:
    - If you're receiving a gift from a family member or friend to use toward your down payment, you'll need a gift letter confirming the source of the funds and that they are a gift, not a loan.

Organizing Your Documents:

To facilitate the pre-approval process, organize your financial documents in an easily accessible and well-labeled folder or digital file. Ensure that all documents are current and complete.

Consult with Your Lender:

Before submitting your documents, consult with your lender or mortgage broker to confirm the specific requirements they have and whether any additional documents are necessary. This proactive approach will help you present a thorough and accurate financial profile to your lender, increasing your chances of a successful mortgage pre-approval.

Comparing Mortgage Options

Once you've been pre-approved for a mortgage, you'll find that there are various mortgage options available to choose from. These options differ in terms of interest rates, terms, down payments, and repayment structures. Selecting the right mortgage is crucial, as it will impact your financial well-being for years to come. In this section, we'll guide you through the process of comparing mortgage options to find the one that best suits your needs and financial goals:

1. Loan Types:
   - Familiarize yourself with the different types of mortgage loans available. Common options include fixed-rate mortgages, adjustable-rate mortgages (ARMs), FHA loans, VA loans, and USDA loans.

2. Interest Rates:
   - Compare interest rates offered by different lenders and mortgage products. Fixed-rate mortgages offer consistent interest rates over the life of the loan, while ARMs may have lower initial rates that adjust periodically.

3. Loan Term:
   - Decide on the loan term that aligns with your financial objectives. Common terms are 15 years and 30 years, but other options may be available. Shorter terms typically have higher monthly payments but lower overall interest costs.

4. Down Payment:
   - Determine the down payment requirement for each loan type. Some loans, like VA and USDA loans, offer low or zero down payment options, while others may require a more substantial upfront payment.

5. Private Mortgage Insurance (PMI):
   - If your down payment is less than 20% of the home's purchase price, you may need to pay PMI. Compare the cost of PMI across different loan options and lenders.

6. Monthly Payment:
   - Calculate and compare the estimated monthly payments for each mortgage option, considering principal, interest, property taxes, homeowners insurance, and any other applicable costs.

7. Total Interest Paid:
   - Evaluate the total interest you'll pay over the life of each loan option. This can help you understand the long-term cost of each mortgage.

8. Rate Lock Policies:
   - Inquire about rate lock policies offered by lenders. A rate lock guarantees your interest rate for a specified period, protecting you from rate increases during that time.

9. Closing Costs:
   - Compare estimated closing costs, which can include origination fees, appraisal fees, title insurance, and other expenses. Some lenders may offer lower closing costs in exchange for a slightly higher interest rate.

10. Prepayment Penalties:
    - Check for any prepayment penalties or restrictions. Some loans may charge fees for paying off the mortgage early.

11. Customer Service and Reputation:
    - Research the reputation and customer service of potential lenders. Read reviews, seek

recommendations, and assess their responsiveness and transparency.

12. Loan Approval Process:
   - Understand the loan approval process, including the lender's timeline and requirements for document submission and underwriting.

13. Comparative Analysis:
   - Create a spreadsheet or table to compare key features of each mortgage option, including interest rates, loan terms, monthly payments, and total costs over time.

14. Consult with a Mortgage Professional:
   - Consult with a mortgage professional or financial advisor to review your options and receive personalized recommendations based on your financial situation and goals.

15. Future Financial Goals:
   - Consider how each mortgage option aligns with your long-term financial goals, such as retirement planning, saving for education, or investment strategies.

Choosing the right mortgage is a significant decision that requires careful consideration of your financial situation and objectives. By comparing mortgage options thoroughly and seeking expert advice, you can make an informed choice that not only suits your current needs but also sets you on a path to financial success in the future.

Understanding Interest Rates

Interest rates play a pivotal role in the world of finance, particularly in the context of mortgages and home buying. As a prospective homeowner, it's essential to grasp the fundamentals of interest rates and their impact on your mortgage. In this section, we'll delve into the concept of interest rates, explore how they affect your mortgage, and provide insights to help you make informed decisions:

What Are Interest Rates?

Interest rates represent the cost of borrowing money or the return on investment for lending money. They are expressed as a percentage and can be either fixed or variable (adjustable). Here are key points to understand about interest rates:

1. Fixed Interest Rates:
   - Fixed interest rates remain constant throughout the life of the loan. Monthly mortgage payments do not change, providing predictability and stability.

2. Variable (Adjustable) Interest Rates:
   - Variable interest rates, often seen in adjustable-rate mortgages (ARMs), can change periodically based on specific indexes and margins. Payments may fluctuate, potentially increasing over time.

3. Prime Rate and Federal Funds Rate:
   - Mortgage interest rates are influenced by broader economic factors, including the prime rate and federal funds rate, which are set by central banks like the Federal Reserve.

How Interest Rates Impact Your Mortgage:

Interest rates significantly affect the overall cost of your mortgage and your monthly payments. Here's how they impact your homebuying journey:

1. Monthly Payments:
   - A higher interest rate results in higher monthly mortgage payments for the same loan amount. Conversely, a lower rate leads to lower monthly payments.

2. Total Interest Paid:
   - Over the life of the loan, the interest rate determines the total amount of interest you'll pay. Lower rates mean less interest paid in the long run.

3. Affordability:
   - Interest rates impact the amount you can borrow and the price range of homes you can consider. Lower rates may make higher-priced homes more affordable.

4. Loan Approval:
   - Interest rates also affect your eligibility for a mortgage. A lower rate can help you qualify for a larger loan, while a higher rate may limit your borrowing capacity.

5. Refinancing Opportunities:
   - Interest rate movements create opportunities to refinance your mortgage. If rates drop significantly, refinancing at a lower rate can save you money on interest payments.

Factors Influencing Mortgage Interest Rates:

Several factors influence mortgage interest rates, including:

1. Economic Conditions:
   - Economic indicators like inflation, employment rates, and GDP growth influence interest rate decisions by central banks.

2. Central Bank Policies:
   - Central banks, such as the Federal Reserve in the United States, set short-term interest rates to control inflation and stimulate or slow down economic growth.

3. Creditworthiness:
   - Your credit score and credit history play a crucial role in the interest rate you qualify for. Higher credit scores typically secure lower rates.

4. Loan Term:
   - Shorter-term loans generally come with lower interest rates compared to longer-term loans.

5. Market Conditions:
   - Supply and demand in the mortgage market can impact rates. A competitive market may lead to lower rates.

6. Global Factors:
   - Global economic events and geopolitical stability can influence interest rates.

Understanding interest rates is vital for making informed decisions about your mortgage. As you explore mortgage options, consider how interest rates align with your budget, financial goals, and risk tolerance. Keep an eye on market trends and consult with mortgage professionals to secure the best possible rate for your home purchase.

Chapter 5: The House-Hunting Process

The moment has arrived. You've completed the essential steps of assessing your financial readiness, securing pre-approval for a mortgage, and comparing mortgage options. Now, you're ready to embark on the exciting and rewarding journey of finding your dream home. Chapter 5 marks the beginning of the house-hunting process—a phase filled with anticipation, exploration, and important decisions.

The House-Hunting Journey:

House hunting isn't just about finding a place to live; it's about discovering the space that will become your sanctuary, the backdrop to your life's memorable moments, and the foundation of your future. In this chapter, we'll guide you through the intricacies of the house-hunting process and provide you with valuable insights to make this adventure as enjoyable and successful as possible.

A Roadmap to Success:

In the upcoming sections, you'll find detailed information and tips on every aspect of house hunting, including:

- Defining Your Preferences: Identifying your must-haves, nice-to-haves, and deal-breakers to create a clear vision of your ideal home.
- Searching for Properties: Exploring various sources, from real estate websites to open houses and local networks, to discover available properties.
- Property Viewings: Making the most of your property viewings by asking the right questions and assessing each potential home objectively.
- Taking Notes and Photos: Keeping a record of your impressions, thoughts, and concerns to aid in the decision-making process.
- Creating a Shortlist: Narrowing down your choices to a select few properties that meet your criteria and deserve further consideration.
- Comparing Properties: Evaluating your shortlist based on a comprehensive set of factors, including location, condition, price, and potential for customization.
- The Art of Negotiation: Understanding the negotiation process and strategies to secure your chosen property at the best possible terms.
- The Due Diligence Phase: Conducting inspections, appraisals, and final checks to ensure the property is a sound investment.
- Closing the Deal: The final steps leading to home ownership, including the closing process, signing documents, and receiving the keys to your new home.
- Moving In: Tips and guidance for a smooth transition into your new home, from packing and hiring movers to settling in and personalizing your space.

A Journey of Discovery:

The house-hunting process is not just about bricks and mortar; it's about discovering the place where you'll build your life, create memories, and pursue your dreams. It's a journey filled with emotions, choices, and anticipation. And, ultimately, it's about finding the place that you'll proudly call home.

So, as we embark on this chapter together, prepare yourself for the exhilarating adventure of house hunting. Whether you're a first-time buyer or an experienced homeowner, the insights and knowledge you'll gain in this chapter will equip you to navigate the real estate market with confidence and enthusiasm. Let the search for your dream home begin!

The First Viewing

The moment has arrived. After weeks or even months of preparation, you're about to step into a potential new home for the very first time. The first viewing is an exhilarating experience—a mix of excitement, curiosity, and the prospect of finding the place where your future will unfold. In this section, we'll guide you through the essential aspects of making the most out of your first property viewing:

1. Prepare in Advance:
   - Review the property details and features before your visit. Familiarize yourself with the property's specifications and any unique selling points.

2. Bring a Checklist:
   - Create a checklist of your must-have features and preferences. This will help you objectively evaluate the property and ensure it aligns with your priorities.

3. Arrive Early:
   - Arriving a bit early gives you the opportunity to explore the neighborhood and get a feel for the surroundings before you step inside.

4. Observe the Exterior:
   - Begin by inspecting the property's exterior. Assess the condition of the roof, siding, landscaping, and any outdoor amenities like a patio or pool.

5. Check Curb Appeal:
   - Consider the property's curb appeal and its potential to make a positive first impression on visitors.

6. Examine the Neighborhood:
   - Take a stroll around the neighborhood to gauge the ambiance, proximity to amenities, and overall vibe of the area.

7. Enter with an Open Mind:
   - Approach the viewing with an open mind. Don't let minor imperfections deter you from seeing the property's potential.

8. Inspect Room by Room:
   - Methodically explore each room. Pay attention to details like lighting, ventilation, and layout. Check for signs of wear and tear or needed repairs.

9. Visualize Your Life There:
   - Try to envision your daily life in the space. Imagine how your furniture and belongings would fit

and how the layout suits your lifestyle.

10. Ask Questions:
   - Don't hesitate to ask the real estate agent questions. Inquire about the property's history, recent renovations, and any specific details not covered in the listing.

11. Take Photos and Notes:
   - Capture the details with photos and take notes during your viewing. This will help you remember each property's unique features and your impressions.

12. Check for Issues:
   - Look for any potential issues, such as water damage, structural concerns, or signs of pests. These may affect your decision-making process.

13. Assess Natural Light:
   - Pay attention to the amount of natural light in each room. Adequate light can greatly influence your living experience.

14. Consider Storage Space:
   - Evaluate storage options, including closets, cabinets, and garage space. Sufficient storage is essential for an organized home.

15. Imagine Future Updates:
   - Think about any updates or renovations you might want to make in the future and whether the property allows for these changes.

16. Take Your Time:
   - Don't rush through the viewing. Spend enough time exploring the property to ensure you have a comprehensive understanding.

17. Leave Feedback:
   - Provide feedback to the real estate agent after the viewing. This will help them refine their search and identify properties that better match your preferences.

The first viewing is an exciting step in your house-hunting journey. It's a chance to see the potential of a property and to gauge whether it feels like the right fit for you. Remember that it's normal to view several properties before finding "the one." By staying organized, asking questions, and considering your priorities, you'll be better equipped to make informed decisions as you continue your search for your dream home.

Keeping an Open Mind

In the quest to find your dream home, one of the most valuable attributes you can possess is an open mind. While it's important to have clear criteria and specific preferences for your future home, being open-minded allows you to explore a broader range of possibilities and seize opportunities you might not have initially considered. Here are some compelling reasons to keep an open mind throughout the house-hunting process:

1. Discovery of Hidden Gems:

- Some properties may not fully align with your initial checklist but could surprise you with unique features or potential. Keeping an open mind allows you to discover hidden gems that might become your ideal home.

2. Adaptation to Market Changes:
   - Real estate markets can be dynamic, and inventory may change rapidly. Being open-minded enables you to adapt to market conditions and seize opportunities that align with your budget and goals.

3. Potential for Customization:
   - A property that doesn't perfectly match your vision may offer the potential for customization and renovation. An open mind can help you see the possibilities for turning a house into your dream home.

4. Broader Range of Neighborhoods:
   - Exploring different neighborhoods with an open mind can reveal areas you hadn't considered before. You might find a neighborhood that offers unexpected advantages or a better fit for your lifestyle.

5. Flexibility on Minor Preferences:
   - Minor details, such as paint colors, fixtures, or landscaping, can often be modified to align with your preferences. An open-minded approach allows you to focus on the property's fundamental qualities.

6. Overcoming Initial Impressions:
   - Sometimes, a property may not make the best first impression but has potential upon closer inspection. Give properties a fair chance by exploring them thoroughly.

7. Room for Negotiation:
   - Being open-minded during negotiations can lead to favorable terms and conditions. Sellers may be more willing to accommodate your requests if they sense your willingness to compromise.

8. Avoiding Missed Opportunities:
   - Rigidity in your preferences may cause you to overlook properties that, with minor adjustments or updates, could become your dream home. An open mind prevents missed opportunities.

9. Embracing Unique Features:
   - Unique or unconventional features in a property may not align with your initial checklist but can add character and charm to your home. Embrace these distinctive elements.

10. Reducing Stress and Pressure:
    - An open-minded approach can reduce the stress and pressure associated with finding the "perfect" home. You can explore options without feeling overwhelmed by rigid criteria.

11. Staying Open to Advice:
    - Seek advice from real estate professionals and trusted friends or family members. They may offer insights and perspectives that encourage you to broaden your horizons.

12. Emotional Connection:
    - Sometimes, a property may resonate with you on an emotional level, even if it doesn't meet all your criteria. An open mind allows you to consider these emotional connections.

While it's essential to have a clear sense of your priorities and must-haves in a home, maintaining flexibility and an open mind can lead you to unexpected opportunities and a more satisfying home-buying experience. Remember that finding the perfect home often involves a degree of compromise and creativity, and it's the journey of exploration that ultimately leads to discovering your ideal place to call home.

Making an Offer

You've found a property that ticks many of your boxes and feels like a potential dream home. Now, it's time to take the next step: making an offer. This pivotal stage in the house-hunting process requires careful consideration and strategic planning. Here's a comprehensive guide to help you navigate the process of making an offer on a property:

1. Consult Your Real Estate Agent:
   - Before drafting an offer, consult with your real estate agent. They'll provide insights into the local market, recent sales, and the property's value, helping you determine a competitive offer price.

2. Review Comparable Sales:
   - Research recent sales of similar properties in the area (comparable sales or "comps"). These sales can serve as benchmarks for pricing your offer.

3. Consider Market Conditions:
   - Take into account the current state of the real estate market. In a seller's market, where demand exceeds supply, you may need to submit a stronger offer to compete with other buyers.

4. Set an Offer Price:
   - Decide on the offer price you're comfortable with. Your real estate agent can help you strike a balance between affordability and competitiveness.

5. Include Earnest Money:
   - Earnest money, also known as a good faith deposit, is a sum of money that demonstrates your commitment to the purchase. It's typically held in an escrow account until the sale closes.

6. Specify Financing Details:
   - Outline the financing terms, including the type of mortgage (e.g., conventional, FHA, VA) and the down payment amount.

7. Set the Closing Date:
   - Choose a realistic closing date that aligns with your lender's timeline and allows ample time for inspections and appraisals.

8. Include Contingencies:
   - Contingencies protect your interests as a buyer. Common contingencies include the financing contingency (approval of the mortgage), inspection contingency (satisfactory inspection results), and appraisal contingency (property appraisal matches the offer price).

9. Offer Expiration Date:
   - Specify an expiration date for your offer to prompt the seller to respond within a reasonable

timeframe.

10. Attach a Personal Letter:
   - In some cases, a personal letter to the seller expressing your appreciation for the property and your intentions can make your offer stand out.

11. Review the Terms and Conditions:
   - Carefully review all terms and conditions with your real estate agent before submitting the offer. Ensure that your offer aligns with your budget and preferences.

12. Submit the Offer:
   - Once your offer is finalized, your real estate agent will submit it to the seller or the seller's agent. Be prepared to provide any additional documentation requested by the seller.

13. Negotiation Phase:
   - The seller may respond to your offer with a counteroffer. This back-and-forth negotiation process can involve adjustments to the offer price, contingencies, or other terms.

14. Acceptance or Rejection:
   - The seller can choose to accept, reject, or counter your offer. If your offer is accepted, the house is considered "under contract," and you move on to the due diligence phase.

15. Due Diligence:
   - During this phase, you'll conduct inspections, appraisals, and any necessary investigations to ensure the property meets your expectations.

16. Closing Process:
   - Once due diligence is completed, you'll proceed to the closing process, which involves finalizing the mortgage, signing documents, and transferring ownership.

17. Prepare for Moving:
   - As the closing date approaches, start planning your move, including packing, hiring movers, and notifying utility providers of the upcoming change.

Making an offer on a property is a pivotal moment in your homebuying journey. It's a step that requires careful consideration, research, and strategic planning. With the guidance of your real estate agent and a well-prepared offer, you can increase your chances of securing the home of your dreams at a price and terms that align with your goals.

Negotiating the Deal

Negotiating the deal is an essential part of the homebuying process that allows you to secure favorable terms, align the purchase with your budget, and address any concerns or contingencies. Effective negotiation requires a strategic approach and clear communication. Here's a step-by-step guide to help you navigate the negotiation process successfully:

1. Review the Seller's Response:
   - When the seller responds to your initial offer, carefully review their counteroffer or acceptance. Pay attention to any changes in price, terms, or contingencies.

2. Consult Your Real Estate Agent:
   - Seek advice from your real estate agent, who can provide insights into the seller's response and the best strategy for your next move.

3. Evaluate the Counteroffer:
   - Assess the seller's counteroffer to determine whether it aligns with your budget and expectations. Consider the reasons behind any changes and their impact on the overall deal.

4. Prepare Your Response:
   - Based on your evaluation, prepare a thoughtful and well-considered response. Address any concerns or issues raised in the counteroffer.

5. Maintain Effective Communication:
   - Keep communication open and professional. Effective negotiation requires clear and respectful dialogue between all parties involved.

6. Be Prepared to Compromise:
   - Understand that negotiation often involves compromise. Identify areas where you are willing to make concessions while protecting your core priorities.

7. Set Limits:
   - Determine your limits in terms of price, contingencies, and terms. Knowing your boundaries helps you negotiate confidently and avoid overstretching your budget.

8. Focus on Win-Win Solutions:
   - Strive for a win-win outcome that benefits both you and the seller. Negotiation doesn't have to be adversarial; it can be a collaborative process.

9. Consider Non-Price Factors:
   - Negotiation isn't limited to price. Non-price factors, such as closing date, repairs, or concessions, can also be negotiated to create a mutually beneficial agreement.

10. Be Patient:
    - Negotiation may involve multiple rounds of offers and counteroffers. Be patient and maintain a constructive approach throughout the process.

11. Consult Legal and Financial Advisors:
    - If needed, consult with legal and financial advisors to ensure that the negotiation aligns with your legal and financial interests.

12. Stay Informed About Market Conditions:
    - Stay updated on the local real estate market and any changes that may impact your negotiation. This knowledge can be a valuable asset.

13. Consider Walk-Away Points:
    - Determine at what point you would be willing to walk away from the deal if the negotiation doesn't meet your minimum requirements.

14. Seek Solutions to Contingencies:
   - If contingencies are a point of negotiation, work collaboratively to find solutions that satisfy both parties while protecting your interests.

15. Finalize the Agreement:
   - Once both parties reach a mutually acceptable agreement, ensure that all terms and conditions are clearly documented in writing.

16. Due Diligence and Closing:
   - Continue with due diligence activities, such as inspections and appraisals, to ensure the property meets your expectations. As the closing date approaches, complete any remaining tasks to finalize the transaction.

Negotiating the deal is an art that requires a balance of assertiveness, patience, and diplomacy. By approaching the negotiation process strategically, staying well-informed, and maintaining effective communication, you can navigate the intricacies of real estate negotiation with confidence and secure a home that meets your needs and aligns with your financial goals.

Chapter 6: The Home Inspection

Congratulations! You've made progress in your journey toward home ownership, and you're now one step closer to calling a property your own. As you delve deeper into the process, the importance of conducting a thorough home inspection cannot be overstated. Chapter 6 explores the critical phase of the home inspection—a comprehensive evaluation of the property's condition and structure.

The Significance of a Home Inspection:

A home is more than just walls and floors; it's an investment in your future and a sanctuary for your family. The home inspection is your opportunity to uncover any hidden issues, potential hazards, or necessary repairs that may impact your decision to proceed with the purchase. It's a vital step in ensuring that your new home is a safe and sound investment.

What to Expect in this Chapter:

In the pages that follow, we'll guide you through the essential aspects of the home inspection process:

- Selecting a Qualified Inspector: Learn how to choose a reputable and experienced home inspector who can provide a comprehensive evaluation of the property.

- The Inspection Process: Explore the step-by-step process of the home inspection, from the roof to the foundation, and understand what inspectors look for in each area.

- Common Issues and Red Flags: Gain insights into common issues that may arise during the inspection and how to interpret red flags.

- Additional Inspections: Discover specialized inspections, such as radon, termite, mold, and sewer inspections, which may be necessary depending on the property and location.

- Understanding Inspection Reports: Learn how to read and interpret inspection reports, and understand the implications of the findings.

- Negotiating Repairs or Credits: Explore how to address any issues discovered during the inspection, including negotiating repairs, credits, or adjustments to the purchase agreement.

- Considering the Inspection in Your Decision: Understand how the inspection results factor into your decision to move forward with the purchase or reevaluate your options.

- Preparing for Closing: As you move closer to closing, prepare for the final steps, including addressing any outstanding inspection-related items and finalizing your financing.

A thorough home inspection is not just about uncovering potential problems; it's about empowering you with knowledge and ensuring that your investment aligns with your expectations. By the end of this chapter, you'll be well-equipped to navigate the home inspection process confidently and make informed decisions that will lead you closer to home ownership.

So, let's dive into Chapter 6 and embark on the enlightening journey of the home inspection—a pivotal phase that brings you one step closer to realizing your dream of owning a home that's safe, secure, and truly your own.

The Purpose of a Home Inspection

A home inspection serves as a critical checkpoint in the homebuying process, offering invaluable insights into the condition and structural integrity of a property. Its primary purpose is to provide you, the prospective homeowner, with a comprehensive understanding of the property's strengths, weaknesses, and potential issues. Let's explore the key purposes of a home inspection:

1. Identify Deficiencies and Issues:
   - A home inspection aims to identify any existing deficiencies, defects, or safety concerns within the property. This includes issues related to the foundation, structure, electrical, plumbing, HVAC systems, roofing, and more.

2. Assess Overall Condition:
   - The inspector assesses the overall condition of the property, providing you with a detailed report on the state of various components and systems. This information helps you gauge the property's maintenance needs.

3. Uncover Hidden Problems:
   - Home inspectors are trained to detect hidden problems or issues that may not be apparent during a casual viewing. They use specialized tools and knowledge to uncover potential problems that could affect your future living experience.

4. Safety Evaluation:
   - Safety is paramount. A home inspection evaluates the safety of the property, highlighting any immediate hazards or issues that could pose a risk to occupants.

5. Educational Opportunity:

- The inspection process offers you an educational opportunity to learn about the property's systems and maintenance requirements. You can ask questions and gain insights into how to care for your future home.

6. Decision-Making Tool:
   - Armed with the inspection report, you can make informed decisions about whether to proceed with the purchase, renegotiate the terms, or potentially walk away if the issues are insurmountable.

7. Negotiation Leverage:
   - The inspection report can be used as a negotiation tool. If significant issues are identified, you can negotiate with the seller for repairs, credits, or adjustments to the purchase agreement.

8. Plan for Future Maintenance:
   - Understanding the condition of the property allows you to plan for future maintenance and repairs, helping you budget effectively for home ownership.

9. Peace of Mind:
   - Ultimately, a home inspection provides you with peace of mind. It ensures that you are making an informed and confident decision about one of the most significant investments of your life.

10. Protection of Investment:
    - For lenders, a satisfactory home inspection report provides assurance that the property is a sound investment and that the buyer is making a prudent decision, reducing the risk of loan defaults.

In summary, a home inspection serves the dual purpose of safeguarding your interests as a buyer and helping you make an informed decision about a property's suitability for your needs. It's a critical step in the homebuying process, offering clarity, transparency, and peace of mind as you move closer to realizing your home ownership dreams.

Finding a Qualified Home Inspector

Selecting a qualified home inspector is a crucial step in ensuring a thorough and reliable evaluation of the property you intend to purchase. A skilled and experienced inspector can uncover hidden issues, provide valuable insights, and help you make an informed decision. Here's a guide on how to find a qualified home inspector:

1. Seek Recommendations:
   - Start by asking your real estate agent, friends, family, or colleagues for recommendations. Real estate professionals often have trusted inspectors they've worked with before.

2. Check Licensing and Certification:
   - Research the licensing and certification requirements for home inspectors in your state or region. Ensure that the inspector you choose meets these requirements.

3. Verify Professional Memberships:
   - Many reputable home inspectors are members of professional organizations such as the American Society of Home Inspectors (ASHI) or the National Association of Home Inspectors (NAHI). Verify if your potential inspector holds any relevant memberships.

4. Review Qualifications:
   - Examine the qualifications and credentials of the inspector, including their education, training, and years of experience in the field.

5. Request Sample Reports:
   - Ask for sample inspection reports from potential inspectors. A well-organized and detailed report is an indicator of their thoroughness and professionalism.

6. Read Reviews and Testimonials:
   - Look for online reviews and testimonials from previous clients. Reading about others' experiences can provide insight into the inspector's reliability and performance.

7. Interview Potential Inspectors:
   - Conduct interviews with potential inspectors. Ask about their inspection process, the time it takes to complete an inspection, and any additional services they offer.

8. Ask for References:
   - Request references from past clients. Contact these references to inquire about their satisfaction with the inspector's services.

9. Check for Errors and Omissions Insurance:
   - Ensure that the inspector carries errors and omissions (E&O) insurance. This insurance provides coverage in case of oversight or errors during the inspection.

10. Inquire About Additional Services:
    - If you have specific concerns, such as radon, mold, or termite issues, inquire whether the inspector can provide additional specialized inspections or can recommend experts in those areas.

11. Attend the Inspection:
    - Whenever possible, attend the inspection yourself. This allows you to ask questions, seek clarification, and gain a better understanding of the property's condition.

12. Ask About Reporting Methods:
    - Inquire about the inspector's reporting methods. Modern inspectors often use digital reports with photos, which can be more comprehensive and easier to understand.

13. Check Availability and Scheduling:
    - Ensure that the inspector's availability aligns with your timeline for the property purchase. Discuss scheduling options and flexibility.

14. Compare Costs:
    - While cost should not be the sole factor in your decision, compare the fees charged by different inspectors. Be wary of significantly lower prices, as they may indicate lack of experience or thoroughness.

15. Trust Your Instincts:
    - Ultimately, trust your instincts. Choose an inspector with whom you feel comfortable and confident in their abilities.

Selecting a qualified home inspector is a vital investment in your future home. Take your time to research and evaluate potential inspectors thoroughly. By choosing a qualified professional, you can ensure a thorough and reliable assessment of the property, providing you with the knowledge and confidence needed to make an informed homebuying decision.

Common Issues Found in Home Inspections

A home inspection is a comprehensive evaluation of a property's condition and systems. During this process, inspectors often uncover various issues, some of which may require attention or negotiation with the seller. While every property is unique, certain issues tend to be more commonly found during home inspections. Here are some of the common issues you may encounter:

1. Roofing Problems:
  - Roofing issues such as missing or damaged shingles, leaks, or signs of wear and tear are frequently identified during inspections. Roof repairs or replacements may be necessary.

2. Structural Concerns:
  - Structural issues, including foundation cracks, settlement, or improper framing, can impact the property's stability and safety. Structural repairs may be required.

3. Plumbing Leaks or Deficiencies:
  - Leaking pipes, dripping faucets, faulty water heaters, or inadequate water pressure are commonly discovered plumbing issues. These issues may affect the property's water supply and drainage.

4. Electrical Problems:
  - Electrical issues such as outdated wiring, overloaded circuits, or faulty outlets can pose safety hazards. Electrical upgrades or repairs may be needed.

5. HVAC System Deficiencies:
  - Problems with the heating, ventilation, and air conditioning (HVAC) system, such as inadequate heating or cooling, malfunctioning components, or poor maintenance, are frequently identified.

6. Mold and Mildew:
  - Inspectors may find signs of mold or mildew, often in damp areas like basements or bathrooms. Mold remediation may be necessary for health and safety reasons.

7. Termites and Pest Infestations:
  - Evidence of termites or other pest infestations can be a major concern. Extermination and repairs may be required to address the issue.

8. Inadequate Insulation:
  - Inadequate insulation in the attic or walls can lead to energy inefficiency and temperature control problems. Additional insulation may be recommended.

9. Water Damage and Moisture Issues:
  - Water damage, moisture intrusion, or signs of water stains on walls and ceilings can indicate leaks or improper drainage. Repairs and waterproofing may be necessary.

10. Aging or Faulty Appliances:

- Aging or malfunctioning appliances, such as water heaters, furnaces, or kitchen appliances, may require replacement or repairs.

11. Environmental Hazards:
   - Inspectors may identify environmental hazards like radon gas, lead-based paint, asbestos, or unsafe levels of carbon monoxide. Mitigation or abatement may be necessary.

12. Crawl Space and Attic Issues:
   - Issues in crawl spaces or attics, such as poor ventilation, insulation problems, or signs of pests, may need attention to maintain the property's integrity.

13. Drainage and Grading Problems:
   - Inadequate drainage or grading that directs water toward the property can lead to moisture issues and potential damage. Corrective measures may be required.

14. Safety Concerns:
   - Safety hazards like missing handrails, improper electrical installations, or defective smoke detectors may be highlighted during inspections.

15. Code Compliance Issues:
   - Non-compliance with building codes or safety regulations may be identified. Bringing the property up to code may be necessary.

Keep in mind that the severity of these issues can vary, and not all homes will have the same problems. The goal of a home inspection is to provide you with a comprehensive understanding of the property's condition, allowing you to make informed decisions about whether to proceed with the purchase and how to address any identified issues with the seller or through negotiations.

Negotiating Repairs and Credits

Once the home inspection is complete, you'll receive a detailed report outlining any issues or deficiencies found in the property. Depending on the findings, you may need to negotiate with the seller to address these concerns before finalizing the purchase. Negotiating repairs and credits is a crucial step in ensuring that the property meets your expectations and is in the condition you require. Here's a guide on how to navigate this process effectively:

1. Review the Inspection Report:
   - Carefully review the home inspection report with your real estate agent. Identify the issues that are most important to you and prioritize them based on their significance and potential cost.

2. Determine What to Request:
   - Decide whether you'll request repairs to be completed by the seller before closing or if you'll ask for a credit to cover the cost of addressing the issues yourself after the purchase.

3. Consult Your Real Estate Agent:
   - Work closely with your real estate agent to develop a negotiation strategy. They can provide valuable insights into the local market and advise you on the best approach.

4. Get Repair Estimates:

- If you plan to request repairs, obtain estimates from qualified contractors or specialists to provide an accurate assessment of the costs involved.

5. Submit Your Request:
   - Draft a clear and concise request for repairs or credits. Include the specific issues, recommended remedies, and a reasonable timeline for resolution.

6. Consider a Seller's Response:
   - Be prepared for the seller's response, which can include accepting your request, rejecting it, or proposing alternatives. Negotiation is often a back-and-forth process.

7. Be Open to Compromise:
   - Be open to compromise during negotiations. While you may want all issues addressed, the seller may be willing to address some but not all of them.

8. Prioritize Safety and Structural Issues:
   - Safety and structural issues should be a top priority. Ensure that any issues affecting the property's safety or integrity are addressed appropriately.

9. Negotiate Credits for Minor Repairs:
   - For minor repairs or issues that you can handle yourself, consider negotiating for a credit instead of requesting the seller to complete the repairs. This can simplify the process.

10. Request Documentation:
    - Request documentation or receipts for any completed repairs or work carried out by the seller to ensure that the agreed-upon repairs are done satisfactorily.

11. Finalize the Agreement:
    - Once both parties agree on the repairs or credits, ensure that the details are documented in an addendum to the purchase agreement. This formalizes the agreement and makes it legally binding.

12. Inspect Repairs:
    - Before closing, schedule a final walkthrough to inspect any repairs completed by the seller to ensure they meet your expectations and the agreed-upon standards.

13. Adjust Closing Costs:
    - If you receive credits for repairs, your closing costs may be adjusted accordingly. Ensure that the credit is reflected correctly in the final settlement statement.

14. Plan for Future Repairs:
    - Keep in mind that not all issues may be addressed during negotiations. Plan for future repairs and maintenance to ensure the property remains in good condition.

Negotiating repairs and credits is a pivotal part of the homebuying process that allows you to address any issues discovered during the inspection. Effective negotiation involves clear communication, a willingness to compromise, and a focus on achieving a mutually satisfactory outcome. By working closely with your real estate agent and the seller, you can ensure that the property meets your expectations and is a sound investment for your future.

Chapter 7: Finalizing Your Mortgage

You've navigated through the process of finding your dream home, conducting inspections, and negotiating terms with the seller. Now, it's time to take the crucial step of finalizing your mortgage—the financial cornerstone of your home ownership journey. In this chapter, we'll delve into the essential aspects of securing your mortgage, ensuring you're well-prepared to make one of the most significant financial commitments of your life.

The Importance of Finalizing Your Mortgage:

A mortgage is more than just a loan; it's the means by which you'll make your dream of home ownership a reality. Finalizing your mortgage is a pivotal moment in your journey, one that demands careful consideration, attention to detail, and financial planning. This chapter aims to provide you with the knowledge and guidance you need to navigate the mortgage process confidently.

What to Expect in this Chapter:

In the pages that follow, we'll explore the critical components of finalizing your mortgage:

- Understanding Mortgage Types: Gain insights into various mortgage options and their features, allowing you to choose the one that aligns with your financial goals and lifestyle.

- The Mortgage Application Process: Navigate the mortgage application process with a clear understanding of the required documents, credit checks, and lender requirements.

- Mortgage Pre-Approval and Prequalification: Learn the distinctions between mortgage pre-approval and prequalification, and discover their advantages in the homebuying process.

- Loan Documentation and Verification: Understand the importance of providing accurate financial documentation and the verification process lenders use to assess your creditworthiness.

- Interest Rates and Terms: Explore the factors that influence mortgage interest rates and terms, helping you secure a mortgage that fits your budget.

- Closing Costs and Fees: Prepare for the costs associated with finalizing your mortgage, including closing costs and fees, and understand how they impact your budget.

- Mortgage Approval and Underwriting: Learn about the mortgage approval process and the role of underwriters in assessing your loan application.

- The Final Walkthrough: Prepare for the final walkthrough, a crucial step before closing, to ensure the property meets your expectations.

- Securing Homeowners Insurance: Understand the importance of homeowners insurance and how to secure the right coverage for your new home.

- The Closing Process: Navigate the final stages of the mortgage process, including signing documents, transferring ownership, and receiving the keys to your new home.

Finalizing your mortgage is a significant milestone that brings you closer to realizing your dream of home ownership. By the end of this chapter, you'll be well-informed and equipped to make informed decisions about your mortgage, ensuring it aligns with your financial goals and secures the keys to your future home.

So, let's embark on Chapter 7 together—a chapter that will empower you with the knowledge and confidence needed to take this significant step toward home ownership.

The Mortgage Application Process

The mortgage application process is a pivotal step on your journey to home ownership. It's the point at which you formally apply for the financing that will make your dream of owning a home a reality. Understanding and navigating this process effectively is crucial to securing the mortgage that aligns with your financial goals and budget. Here's a comprehensive guide to help you navigate the mortgage application process:

1. Preparation and Financial Assessment:
   - Before you begin the application, assess your financial situation. Review your credit report, gather financial documents, and determine your budget for home ownership.

2. Choose the Right Mortgage:
   - Research and select the type of mortgage that best suits your needs. Common options include fixed-rate mortgages, adjustable-rate mortgages (ARMs), FHA loans, VA loans, and more.

3. Select a Lender:
   - Choose a reputable lender or mortgage broker to work with. Seek recommendations, read reviews, and consider factors such as interest rates, fees, and customer service.

4. Mortgage Pre-Approval vs. Prequalification:
   - Decide whether to pursue mortgage pre-approval or prequalification. Pre-approval provides a more robust commitment from the lender and carries more weight in negotiations.

5. Complete the Application:
   - Fill out the mortgage application provided by your chosen lender. Be prepared to provide personal information, financial details, employment history, and information about the property you intend to purchase.

6. Provide Required Documentation:
   - Gather and submit the necessary documentation, which typically includes pay stubs, W-2s, tax returns, bank statements, and any additional financial records requested by the lender.

7. Credit Check and Verification:
   - The lender will conduct a credit check to assess your creditworthiness. Be prepared for a thorough review of your financial history.

8. Appraisal and Property Evaluation:
   - The lender may order an appraisal to determine the property's value. The appraisal ensures that the property is worth the loan amount.

9. Underwriting and Decision:
   - The underwriter will assess your application, creditworthiness, and the property's appraisal report. They will make a decision regarding your mortgage application.

10. Conditional Approval:
    - If your application is approved with conditions, you may be required to provide additional documentation or address specific issues to meet the lender's requirements.

11. Final Loan Approval:
    - Once all conditions are satisfied, your loan will receive final approval. This step signifies that your mortgage is ready for closing.

12. Locking in Interest Rates:
    - You can choose to lock in your interest rate during the application process to secure the rate offered by the lender. Rate locks typically have expiration dates, so be aware of the timeline.

13. Closing Disclosure:
    - You will receive a Closing Disclosure outlining the final loan terms, interest rate, closing costs, and other financial details. Review this document carefully for accuracy.

14. Closing Preparation:
    - Prepare for the closing by coordinating with your real estate agent, reviewing all documentation, and ensuring you have funds for the down payment and closing costs.

15. The Closing Meeting:
    - Attend the closing meeting, where you'll sign the mortgage documents, transfer ownership, and receive the keys to your new home.

16. Post-Closing:
    - After closing, keep records of your mortgage documents, continue making timely payments, and stay in communication with your lender for any future inquiries or concerns.

Navigating the mortgage application process requires thorough preparation, attention to detail, and clear communication with your lender. By understanding the steps involved and working closely with your real estate agent and lender, you can confidently progress toward securing the financing that will help you achieve your goal of home ownership.

Appraisal and Underwriting

Appraisal and underwriting are critical steps in the mortgage application process, designed to assess the property's value and your creditworthiness. These steps are essential for the lender to determine whether to approve your mortgage application and under what terms. Let's explore these processes in detail:

Appraisal:

An appraisal is an independent assessment of a property's value performed by a licensed appraiser. Its purpose is to ensure that the property's value matches the loan amount requested, providing assurance to the lender that they are making a sound investment. Here's what you need to know about the appraisal process:

- Appraiser Selection: The lender typically selects an appraiser who is experienced and knowledgeable about the local real estate market.

- Property Inspection: The appraiser conducts an on-site inspection of the property, assessing its condition, size, features, and overall appeal.

- Comparative Analysis: The appraiser compares the property to recently sold homes (comps) in the area to determine its fair market value.

- Appraisal Report: After the inspection and analysis, the appraiser prepares an appraisal report, which includes the property's value and the basis for that valuation.

- Impact on Financing: If the appraised value is equal to or higher than the purchase price, it's typically a positive outcome. However, if the appraisal comes in lower than expected, it can impact your financing. You may need to renegotiate with the seller, make a larger down payment, or consider alternative financing options.

Underwriting:

Underwriting is the process by which a lender evaluates your mortgage application and determines whether to approve or deny it. This step also involves assessing your creditworthiness, financial stability, and the property's appraisal report. Here's what you need to know about the underwriting process:

- Initial Review: The underwriter begins by reviewing your application, credit report, and financial documentation. They assess your income, debts, credit history, and employment stability.

- Property Evaluation: The underwriter examines the property's appraisal report to ensure it meets the lender's criteria. They confirm that the property's value justifies the loan amount.

- Conditions and Documentation: If the underwriter identifies any issues or requires additional documentation, they may issue conditional approval. This means you'll need to satisfy specific conditions, such as providing updated financial documents or explanations for certain financial events.

- Verification of Information: The underwriter verifies the accuracy of the information provided in your application and documentation. This includes contacting your employer, reviewing bank statements, and confirming your assets.

- Debt-to-Income Ratio: The underwriter calculates your debt-to-income (DTI) ratio, which is a key factor in the decision. A lower DTI ratio typically makes you a more attractive borrower.

- Credit Analysis: Your credit history and credit score play a significant role in the underwriting process. Lenders use this information to assess your creditworthiness and evaluate the risk of lending to you.

- Final Decision: After a thorough review, the underwriter makes a final decision regarding your mortgage application. They may approve it, deny it, or request additional information.

- Clear to Close: If your application is approved, you will receive a "clear to close" from the underwriter, indicating that the loan is ready for closing. At this point, you're one step closer to home ownership.

The appraisal and underwriting processes are integral to securing a mortgage and purchasing your home. It's crucial to provide accurate information, maintain open communication with your lender, and be prepared for potential challenges that may arise during these stages. By understanding the roles of appraisal and underwriting and being proactive in addressing any issues, you can increase your chances of a successful mortgage approval and a smooth path to home ownership.

Closing Costs and Loan Documents

As you approach the final stages of your homebuying journey, you'll encounter closing costs and loan documents. These are essential aspects of the process, as they involve the financial aspects of your mortgage and the legal transfer of ownership. Here's a detailed look at closing costs and the key loan documents you'll encounter:

Closing Costs:

Closing costs are the fees and expenses associated with finalizing a real estate transaction. They encompass a wide range of charges that buyers and sellers must pay at the closing table. It's important to budget for these costs, as they can significantly impact the amount of money you need to bring to the closing. Here are some common closing costs:

- Loan Origination Fee: Charged by the lender for processing the mortgage application and underwriting the loan.

- Appraisal Fee: The cost of the property appraisal to determine its value.

- Credit Report Fee: The fee for obtaining your credit report during the loan application process.

- Title Insurance: Protects against title defects or disputes and ensures a clear title transfer.

- Title Search Fee: The cost of researching the property's ownership history to identify any issues.

- Home Inspection Fee: If not paid earlier, you may need to cover this cost at closing.

- Property Taxes: A pro-rated amount to cover property taxes for the period you'll own the property.

- Homeowners Insurance: Payment for the first year's premium of your homeowners insurance policy.

- Escrow Account Funding: Funds placed in an escrow account for property taxes, homeowners insurance, and mortgage insurance.

- Recording Fees: The cost to record the new deed and mortgage with the local government.

- Attorney Fees: If an attorney is involved in the closing process.

- Survey Fee: The cost of a property survey, if required.

- Courier and Wire Transfer Fees: Charges for delivering documents and transferring funds.

- Document Preparation Fees: Charges for preparing the necessary legal documents.

Loan Documents:

At the closing table, you'll be presented with a stack of loan documents that require your signature. These documents formalize the mortgage agreement and other legal aspects of the transaction. Here are some of the key loan documents you'll encounter:

- Promissory Note: This document outlines your promise to repay the loan, including details such as the loan amount, interest rate, repayment terms, and consequences of default.

- Deed of Trust or Mortgage: This document serves as collateral for the loan, allowing the lender to take ownership of the property if you fail to repay the mortgage.

- Closing Disclosure (CD): A detailed breakdown of the final terms of your loan, including interest rate, monthly payments, and closing costs. You'll receive this document a few days before closing.

- HUD-1 or Closing Disclosure (CD): A summary of all financial transactions involved in the closing, including a breakdown of closing costs.

- Truth-in-Lending (TIL) Statement: Provides information about the costs of your loan, including the annual percentage rate (APR).

- Mortgage Insurance Documents: If required, documents related to private mortgage insurance (PMI) or mortgage insurance premiums (MIP).

- Escrow Agreement: Details how your escrow account will be managed for property taxes and homeowners insurance.

- Loan Estimate (LE): A document outlining the estimated costs of your loan, including interest rates, monthly payments, and closing costs. You'll receive this document early in the loan application process.

- Notice of Right to Cancel (if applicable): For certain types of loans, this document allows you a specified period to cancel the transaction without penalty.

- Other Disclosures and Agreements: Additional documents that may include federal and state-specific disclosures, lender-specific forms, and legal notices.

It's essential to read and understand each loan document before signing. If you have questions or concerns, don't hesitate to ask your lender or attorney for clarification. Once all documents are signed, and the closing costs are settled, you'll officially become a homeowner, and the keys to your new property will be handed over to you.

Closing Day and Signing Your Mortgage

Closing day is the culmination of your homebuying journey—a day filled with excitement, paperwork, and the realization of your home ownership dream. It's the moment when you officially take possession of your new home and sign the mortgage documents. Here's what you can expect on this pivotal day:

1. Location and Participants:
   - The closing typically takes place at a title company's office, a real estate attorney's office, or another neutral location. The participants may include the buyer, seller, real estate agents, and a representative from the title company or closing attorney.

2. Review of Documents:
   - Before the closing, you'll have the opportunity to review the loan documents, including the Closing Disclosure (CD) and the promissory note. Ensure that you understand the terms, interest rate, and monthly payments.

3. Final Walkthrough:
   - Before heading to the closing, you'll likely conduct a final walkthrough of the property to ensure it's in the condition you expected and that any negotiated repairs have been completed.

4. Payment of Closing Costs:
   - On closing day, you'll be responsible for paying the closing costs, which include fees for the loan origination, title insurance, escrow account, and other expenses. You can usually pay by certified check or wire transfer.

5. Signing Mortgage Documents:
   - The central part of the closing involves signing the mortgage and related documents. These include the promissory note, deed of trust or mortgage, and various disclosures. Be prepared to sign your name numerous times.

6. Transfer of Funds:
   - Once you've signed all the necessary documents, the lender will transfer the funds to the seller, and ownership of the property will be officially transferred to you.

7. Recording of Documents:
   - The signed documents are recorded with the local county recorder's office, officially documenting your ownership of the property.

8. Receipt of Keys:
   - After all documents are signed, and funds are transferred, you'll receive the keys to your new home. Congratulations, you're now a homeowner!

9. Review of Settlement Statement:
   - Before leaving the closing, review the settlement statement (typically the HUD-1 or Closing Disclosure) to ensure that all details, including closing costs and credits, are accurate.

10. Homeowners Insurance and Escrow Account:

- If you have homeowners insurance, you may be required to provide proof of coverage. Your lender will also establish an escrow account for property taxes and insurance premiums.

11. Post-Closing Questions:
   - If you have any questions or concerns after the closing, don't hesitate to reach out to your lender or real estate agent for clarification or assistance.

12. Celebrate Your New Home:
   - After the closing, take some time to celebrate your new home. This is a significant milestone in your life, and you should savor the moment.

Remember that closing day can be both exciting and overwhelming, so it's crucial to be prepared and well-informed. Review your loan documents, ask questions if needed, and ensure that you feel comfortable with the terms and conditions of your mortgage. With everything in order, you can confidently sign your mortgage documents and officially embark on your journey as a homeowner.

Chapter 8: home ownership Responsibilities

Congratulations! You've successfully navigated the homebuying process, secured your mortgage, and now hold the keys to your new home. As you step into this exciting chapter of your life as a homeowner, it's important to understand the responsibilities that come with owning a property. In this chapter, we'll explore the various aspects of home ownership and provide guidance on how to effectively manage your new responsibilities.

The Transition to home ownership:

Becoming a homeowner marks a significant transition in your life. While the sense of pride and accomplishment is undeniable, it's essential to recognize that home ownership entails more than just having a place to call your own. It brings a set of responsibilities that require attention, care, and financial management.

What to Expect in this Chapter:

In the pages that follow, we'll delve into the core responsibilities of home ownership, offering insights and advice on how to navigate each aspect effectively. Here are some of the key topics we'll cover:

- Maintaining Your Property: Learn how to keep your home in good condition through regular maintenance, repairs, and renovations.

- Budgeting and Financial Management: Discover strategies for managing your household budget, including mortgage payments, property taxes, insurance, and utilities.

- Homeowners Association (HOA) Guidelines: Understand the role of HOAs, if applicable, and how to comply with their rules and regulations.

- Property Insurance: Explore the importance of homeowners insurance and how to ensure you have adequate coverage.

- Property Taxes: Learn about property tax assessment and payment, as well as potential tax deductions.

- Energy Efficiency and Sustainability: Explore ways to make your home more energy-efficient and environmentally friendly.

- Home Security: Consider measures to enhance the security of your home and protect your family and belongings.

- Community Involvement: Engage with your local community and build positive relationships with your neighbors.

- Home Improvement Projects: Plan and execute home improvement projects that add value to your property.

- Emergency Preparedness: Prepare for emergencies and natural disasters to safeguard your home and loved ones.

- Home ownership Challenges: Address common challenges that homeowners may face and learn how to overcome them.

This chapter is designed to empower you with knowledge, resources, and practical tips to excel in your role as a homeowner. While home ownership brings responsibilities, it also offers the opportunity to create a space that truly reflects your style, values, and aspirations.

As you embark on this chapter, remember that home ownership is a long-term commitment that can bring immense satisfaction and personal growth. By taking proactive steps to manage your responsibilities and make informed decisions, you can enjoy the benefits of home ownership to the fullest. So, let's dive into Chapter 8, where you'll gain the insights and tools needed to embrace your new role as a responsible and proud homeowner.

Setting Up Utilities and Services

As a new homeowner, one of your first responsibilities is to ensure that your new property is equipped with essential utilities and services. These services are the backbone of a comfortable and functional home. In this section, we'll guide you through the process of setting up utilities and services, making your transition into home ownership a smooth one.

1. Review Existing Services:
   - Start by reviewing any existing utilities and services that the previous homeowner may have had. This includes water, electricity, gas, and trash collection. Ensure that these services are active and in your name.

2. Contact Utility Providers:
   - Contact the local utility providers for the services you need. This may include contacting the city or county for water and sewer services, as well as private companies for gas and electricity.

3. Schedule Service Transfers or New Connections:
   - If the previous homeowner had these services in their name, you'll likely need to transfer the

accounts to your name. Alternatively, if there are new connections required, schedule installation appointments with the providers.

4. Arrange for Trash and Recycling Pickup:
   - Find out the trash and recycling pickup schedule for your area and arrange for bins or containers if they're not already provided.

5. Internet, Cable, and Phone Services:
   - Research and contact providers for internet, cable, and phone services in your area. Compare packages and pricing to choose the options that best suit your needs.

6. Security System Setup:
   - If you plan to install a security system, contact a reputable provider and schedule installation. Ensure that your home is secure and protected.

7. Home Insurance:
   - Confirm that your homeowners insurance policy is active and provides adequate coverage. Notify your insurer of your new address.

8. Emergency Services and 911:
   - Familiarize yourself with local emergency services and the 911 system in your area. Ensure that your address is properly registered with emergency services.

9. Home Maintenance Services:
   - Consider setting up regular home maintenance services, such as lawn care, pest control, or HVAC maintenance, if applicable.

10. Budget for Utility Costs:
    - As you set up utilities and services, factor in the costs into your monthly budget. Utility bills can vary based on usage and location, so be prepared for fluctuations.

11. Automatic Payments:
    - Consider setting up automatic payments for your utility bills to ensure they are paid on time. Many providers offer this convenient option.

12. Home Warranty (if applicable):
    - If your home came with a warranty, review the coverage and contact the warranty company if you encounter any issues covered by the warranty.

13. Notify Service Providers of Address Change:
    - Don't forget to update your address with various service providers, such as your bank, credit card companies, insurance providers, and any subscriptions you have.

14. Energy Efficiency:
    - Consider energy-efficient upgrades to your home, such as LED lighting, programmable thermostats, and energy-efficient appliances, to reduce utility costs.

15. Explore Renewable Energy Options:
    - Research renewable energy options, such as solar panels, to reduce your carbon footprint and

potentially lower your energy bills in the long run.

By proactively setting up utilities and services, you'll ensure that your new home is comfortable, functional, and ready for you to enjoy. Take the time to research and choose providers that offer the best services and pricing for your needs, and don't hesitate to reach out to your real estate agent or neighbors for recommendations and guidance in your new community.

Home Maintenance and Repairs

Owning a home comes with the responsibility of maintaining and occasionally repairing various aspects of your property. Proper home maintenance not only ensures your home's longevity but also contributes to your comfort and safety. In this section, we'll explore the essential aspects of home maintenance and repairs to help you become a proactive and responsible homeowner.

1. Create a Maintenance Schedule:
   - Establish a regular maintenance schedule to stay on top of tasks such as cleaning, inspections, and routine upkeep. Create a calendar with reminders for specific tasks.

2. Inspect Your Home:
   - Conduct regular inspections of your home's exterior and interior. Look for signs of wear and tear, damage, or potential issues. Pay attention to the roof, siding, foundation, plumbing, electrical systems, and HVAC.

3. Seasonal Maintenance:
   - Adjust your maintenance tasks based on the seasons. For example, clean gutters in the fall, service your air conditioning in the spring, and prepare your heating system for winter.

4. HVAC Maintenance:
   - Schedule regular maintenance for your heating, ventilation, and air conditioning (HVAC) system. Change filters as recommended and have a professional service the system annually.

5. Plumbing and Water Systems:
   - Check for leaks, drips, or running toilets. Insulate pipes in cold weather to prevent freezing. Regularly flush the water heater and clean faucet aerators.

6. Electrical Maintenance:
   - Inspect electrical outlets, switches, and circuit breakers for signs of wear or overheating. Replace any damaged components and schedule an electrician for repairs if needed.

7. Roof and Gutters:
   - Inspect your roof for missing or damaged shingles, leaks, or signs of deterioration. Clean gutters and downspouts to prevent clogs and water damage.

8. Exterior Maintenance:
   - Maintain the exterior of your home by cleaning siding, repainting as needed, and addressing any wood rot or pest infestations.

9. Lawn and Landscaping:
   - Keep your yard and landscaping in good condition by mowing the lawn, trimming bushes, and

maintaining irrigation systems.

10. Appliance Maintenance:
   - Regularly clean and maintain appliances such as the refrigerator, dishwasher, oven, and washing machine to extend their lifespan and improve energy efficiency.

11. Safety Checks:
   - Test smoke detectors, carbon monoxide detectors, and fire extinguishers regularly. Replace batteries as needed.

12. Emergency Repairs:
   - Be prepared for unexpected repairs, such as plumbing leaks, electrical issues, or HVAC breakdowns. Have a list of trusted contractors and service providers for emergencies.

13. DIY vs. Professional Repairs:
   - Understand your capabilities and limitations when it comes to DIY repairs. For complex or potentially dangerous tasks, it's often best to hire a professional.

14. Budget for Repairs:
   - Set aside funds in your budget for home repairs and maintenance. Having an emergency fund for unexpected repairs can provide peace of mind.

15. Home Warranty:
   - Consider a home warranty plan that can help cover the costs of certain repairs and replacements.

16. Long-Term Planning:
   - Plan for long-term improvements, such as roof replacements, kitchen renovations, or adding energy-efficient features. Save and budget accordingly.

Proactive home maintenance and prompt repairs are key to preserving your home's value and ensuring your safety and comfort. By staying organized, following a maintenance schedule, and addressing issues as they arise, you'll be better equipped to enjoy the benefits of home ownership while minimizing the stress and costs associated with major repairs.

Insurance and Property Taxes

As a homeowner, it's crucial to understand and manage your insurance and property tax responsibilities. These financial aspects of home ownership play a significant role in safeguarding your investment and ensuring you meet your obligations as a property owner. Let's explore insurance and property taxes in detail:

1. Homeowners Insurance:
   - Homeowners insurance provides protection for your home and personal belongings in the event of damage, theft, or other covered perils. Here's what you need to know:

   - Coverage Types: Understand the types of coverage offered by homeowners insurance, including dwelling coverage, personal property coverage, liability protection, and additional living expenses coverage.

- Policy Limits: Review your policy to understand coverage limits and deductibles. Ensure that your coverage adequately protects your home and possessions.

  - Comparison Shopping: Shop around for homeowners insurance to find the best coverage at a competitive rate. Consider factors like the insurance company's reputation and customer service.

  - Premium Payments: Pay your insurance premiums on time to keep your coverage active. Consider setting up automatic payments for convenience.

  - Home Improvements: Inform your insurance provider about significant home improvements or renovations, as they can impact your coverage needs and premium rates.

  - Claims Process: Familiarize yourself with the claims process, including how to report a claim and what to expect when filing a claim.

2. Property Taxes:
  - Property taxes are levied by your local government and help fund essential services like schools, roads, and public safety. Here's what you should know:

  - Tax Assessment: Understand how your property's value is assessed for tax purposes. Your property's assessed value plays a crucial role in determining your property tax bill.

  - Tax Rate: Be aware of the property tax rate in your area, which can vary depending on your city, county, and school district.

  - Due Dates: Know when property tax payments are due in your locality. Missing payment deadlines can result in penalties and interest charges.

  - Escrow Accounts: If you have a mortgage, your lender may establish an escrow account to collect property tax payments on your behalf. Understand how this arrangement works and review statements for accuracy.

  - Exemptions and Deductions: Explore potential property tax exemptions or deductions for which you may qualify, such as homestead exemptions for primary residences or senior citizen exemptions.

  - Appeals Process: Familiarize yourself with the property tax appeals process in case you believe your property has been overvalued.

3. Budgeting for Insurance and Taxes:
  - Budget for homeowners insurance premiums and property tax payments. Factor these expenses into your monthly or annual budget to ensure you're financially prepared.

4. Homeowners Association (HOA) Fees (if applicable):
  - If you live in an HOA community, be aware of the association fees and how they are allocated, including any portion designated for insurance or property maintenance.

5. Keep Records:
  - Maintain records of insurance policies, premium payments, property tax bills, and any correspondence related to insurance claims or tax assessments.

6. Consult Professionals:
   - Consider consulting with an insurance agent or tax professional to ensure you have the right coverage and understand your property tax obligations.

Managing homeowners insurance and property taxes is essential to protect your home and maintain good standing as a property owner. Stay informed, budget responsibly, and seek professional advice when necessary to navigate these financial aspects of home ownership successfully.

Planning for Future Upgrades

Owning a home is not just about maintaining its current condition; it's also an opportunity to enhance and personalize your living space over time. Planning for future upgrades allows you to improve your home's functionality, aesthetics, and value while aligning with your long-term vision. Here's how to approach planning for future home upgrades:

1. Set Your Goals:
   - Begin by defining your goals and priorities for future upgrades. Consider both immediate needs and long-term aspirations. Do you want to expand your living space, update the kitchen, enhance energy efficiency, or create a beautiful outdoor oasis? Your goals will guide your planning process.

2. Create a Home Improvement Wishlist:
   - Make a list of specific home improvements and upgrades you'd like to undertake in the future. Organize the list by priority and feasibility.

3. Establish a Budget:
   - Determine how much you can allocate for future home upgrades. Consider setting up a dedicated savings account or fund to cover these expenses. A budget will help you prioritize projects and make informed decisions.

4. Research and Prioritize Projects:
   - Research each planned upgrade thoroughly. Gather information on costs, timelines, contractors, and potential return on investment (ROI). Prioritize projects based on your budget and goals.

5. Consider Energy Efficiency:
   - Assess your home's energy efficiency and explore upgrades that can reduce utility bills and environmental impact. These may include upgrading insulation, windows, appliances, or installing solar panels.

6. Maintenance First:
   - Before tackling major upgrades, ensure your home is well-maintained. Address any outstanding repairs, such as roof leaks, plumbing issues, or electrical problems, to prevent further damage.

7. DIY vs. Professional Work:
   - Evaluate your DIY skills and the complexity of each project. Some upgrades may be suitable for DIY efforts, while others require professional contractors. Choose wisely to ensure quality results.

8. Plan for Permits:
   - Be aware of local building codes and permit requirements for the upgrades you plan to undertake.

Factor in permit costs and approval timelines.

9. Phased Approach:
   - Consider a phased approach to larger projects. Divide extensive renovations into manageable stages to spread out costs and minimize disruption to your daily life.

10. Home Equity and Financing Options:
    - Explore financing options for your home upgrades. Home equity loans, lines of credit, or refinancing are potential avenues to access funds for major projects.

11. Consult Professionals:
    - Consult with architects, interior designers, or contractors to get expert advice and estimates for your projects. They can help you refine your plans and identify potential challenges.

12. Resale Value and Personal Enjoyment:
    - Balance your upgrades between improvements that enhance your quality of life and those that add resale value to your home. Finding the right mix can provide both immediate and long-term benefits.

13. Timeframe and Project Scheduling:
    - Establish a timeframe for each upgrade based on your priorities and budget. Create a project schedule to keep track of deadlines and milestones.

14. Persevere Through Challenges:
    - Be prepared for unexpected challenges or delays that may arise during home improvement projects. Flexibility and patience are key when dealing with unforeseen issues.

15. Document Your Progress:
    - Keep records of your home improvement projects, including before-and-after photos, receipts, warranties, and any relevant documentation. This will be useful for future reference and potential resale.

Planning for future upgrades allows you to enhance your home gradually, make informed decisions, and ensure your investment aligns with your long-term vision for your property. Whether you're looking to create a dream kitchen, expand your living space, or increase energy efficiency, a well-thought-out plan will help you achieve your goals and enjoy your home for years to come.

Chapter 9: Moving In and Making It Yours

Welcome to the final chapter of your homebuying journey! You've successfully navigated the process of purchasing a home, tackled important responsibilities, and planned for future upgrades. Now, it's time to make your new house a home—a place that reflects your personality, meets your needs, and provides comfort and happiness for you and your loved ones.

The Transition to Your New Home:

Moving into your new home is an exciting and transformative experience. It's a time for settling in, personalizing your space, and creating lasting memories. In this chapter, we'll explore the essential steps and considerations for making a smooth transition to your new abode and turning it into your ideal sanctuary.

What to Expect in this Chapter:

In the pages that follow, we'll delve into the following aspects of moving in and making your home truly yours:

- Moving Day Essentials: Tips and strategies to plan a stress-free moving day, from packing and logistics to hiring movers and unpacking efficiently.

- Personalizing Your Space: Ideas for infusing your personality and style into your home's decor and design. Discover how to create functional and aesthetically pleasing living spaces.

- Home Organization: Practical tips for organizing your home, including decluttering, establishing storage systems, and maintaining order.

- Settling In: Strategies for acclimating to your new neighborhood and community, building relationships with neighbors, and finding local resources.

- Safety and Security: Measures to enhance the safety and security of your home, such as home security systems, fire safety, and emergency preparedness.

- Entertaining and Hosting: Tips for hosting gatherings, parties, and events in your new home. Explore ways to create a welcoming and enjoyable atmosphere for guests.

- Landscaping and Outdoor Spaces: Ideas for beautifying your outdoor areas, whether you have a backyard, garden, balcony, or patio. Transform your outdoor space into a relaxing retreat.

- Home Maintenance Routines: Establishing a regular home maintenance routine to ensure your property remains in excellent condition.

- Personal Growth and Happiness: The significance of the home in personal growth, happiness, and well-being. How to create a positive and harmonious living environment.

- Reflecting on Your Journey: Take a moment to reflect on your homebuying journey, celebrate your accomplishments, and look ahead to your future in your new home.

Your home is a canvas awaiting your personal touch and creativity. With the insights, advice, and inspiration provided in this chapter, you'll embark on the exciting journey of transforming your new house into a home that mirrors your unique identity and fosters the experiences and memories that matter most to you.

So, let's dive into Chapter 9, where you'll discover the joy of moving in and making your new home truly and unmistakably yours.

Preparing for the Move

Moving to a new home is an exciting but often challenging endeavor. Proper preparation can significantly reduce stress and ensure a smoother transition. In this section, we'll guide you through the essential steps to prepare for your move:

1. Create a Moving Timeline:
   - Start by creating a detailed timeline that outlines all the tasks you need to complete before moving day. This will help you stay organized and on track.

2. Declutter and Downsize:
   - Before packing, go through your belongings and decide what to keep, donate, sell, or discard. Reducing your possessions will make the moving process more manageable and may even save you money on moving expenses.

3. Gather Packing Supplies:
   - Collect packing materials such as cardboard boxes, packing tape, bubble wrap, packing paper, and markers. You can purchase boxes or ask local businesses for spare ones.

4. Label and Organize:
   - Label each box with its contents and the room it belongs to. This makes unpacking easier and helps you locate specific items when needed.

5. Pack Strategically:
   - Start packing early, beginning with items you don't use frequently. Pack room by room, keeping similar items together. Be mindful of fragile items and use proper padding and protection.

6. Essentials Box:
   - Pack a box with essential items you'll need immediately upon arrival at your new home. Include toiletries, medications, important documents, a change of clothes, and any necessary electronics.

7. Notify Service Providers:
   - Contact utility companies, internet and cable providers, and other services to schedule disconnects or transfers to your new address.

8. Update Your Address:
   - Notify the post office, banks, credit card companies, subscriptions, and government agencies of your change of address.

9. Hire Movers or Rent a Truck:
   - Decide whether you'll hire professional movers or rent a moving truck. Obtain quotes and make reservations well in advance.

10. Reserve Elevators and Parking:
    - If you're moving into an apartment or condominium, reserve elevators and parking spaces for the moving day.

11. Arrange for Child and Pet Care:
    - If you have children or pets, arrange for their care on moving day to ensure their safety and minimize disruptions.

12. Dispose of Hazardous Items:
   - Properly dispose of or safely transport hazardous materials, such as chemicals, paint, and propane tanks, according to local regulations.

13. Inventory and Documentation:
   - Create an inventory list of your belongings, complete with photos or videos, for insurance purposes. Keep important documents, such as moving contracts, in a secure folder.

14. Packing Electronics:
   - Take photos of the wiring and connections for your electronics before disconnecting them. Use cable ties or labels to keep cords organized.

15. Moving Day Essentials:
   - Prepare a box with cleaning supplies, trash bags, and basic tools for any last-minute needs on moving day.

16. Final Walkthrough:
   - Before leaving your old home, conduct a final walkthrough to ensure nothing is left behind.

17. Say Goodbye:
   - Take a moment to say goodbye to your old home and reflect on the memories you've created there.

Moving can be a complex process, but with careful planning and organization, you can make it more manageable. Start early, stay organized, and enlist help from friends or professionals if needed. By following these steps, you'll be well-prepared for a successful and stress-free move to your new home.

Unpacking and Organizing

After the excitement of moving to your new home, the next step is unpacking and organizing your belongings. This phase allows you to turn your new house into a comfortable and functional living space. Here's how to efficiently unpack and create an organized home:

1. Prioritize Essentials:
   - Begin by unpacking the essentials box you prepared for moving day. This should contain items like toiletries, medications, important documents, and a change of clothes.

2. Room by Room:
   - Unpack room by room to stay organized and focused. Start with the rooms you'll use immediately, such as the bedroom, bathroom, and kitchen.

3. Furniture Placement:
   - Arrange your furniture in each room according to your floor plan and personal preferences. Consider factors like traffic flow, access to outlets, and the placement of large pieces.

4. Kitchen Setup:
   - Organize your kitchen by placing dishes, utensils, and cookware in accessible locations. Consider using drawer dividers and cabinet organizers to maximize storage space.

5. Bathroom Essentials:
   - Arrange your bathroom essentials like towels, toiletries, and cleaning supplies. Use storage solutions like shower caddies and under-sink organizers.

6. Closet Organization:
   - Hang and fold your clothes in the closet and drawers. Consider using closet organizers and storage bins to keep things tidy.

7. Label Boxes:
   - As you unpack, remove labels from boxes and dispose of them. This can help create a neater and more organized space.

8. Declutter as You Go:
   - As you unpack, evaluate your possessions and consider donating or selling items you no longer need or use.

9. Storage Solutions:
   - Invest in storage solutions like shelves, bins, and baskets to keep items organized. Use clear containers for items that aren't used frequently to easily identify their contents.

10. Home Office Setup:
    - If you have a home office, set it up with your computer, office supplies, and any necessary files or paperwork.

11. Living Room Arrangement:
    - Arrange your living room furniture and entertainment center to create a comfortable and inviting space.

12. Bedroom Comfort:
    - Make your bedroom comfortable by arranging your bed, adding bedding, and organizing your clothing and personal items.

13. Children's Rooms:
    - Set up your children's rooms with their belongings, ensuring safety and accessibility.

14. Garage and Storage Spaces:
    - Organize your garage and storage areas, using shelves, hooks, and storage containers to keep things in order.

15. Decor and Personal Touches:
    - Add personal touches and decor to make your home feel welcoming and reflect your style. Hang artwork, arrange photos, and place decorative items throughout your home.

16. Routine Cleaning:
    - Keep cleaning supplies handy to maintain a clean and tidy home. Regular cleaning routines can help you stay organized and prevent clutter from accumulating.

17. Final Walkthrough:
    - Once you've completed unpacking and organizing, conduct a final walkthrough of your home to

ensure everything is in its place and functioning correctly.

18. Explore Your New Neighborhood:
   - Take breaks from unpacking to explore your new neighborhood and community. Visit local stores, parks, and amenities to get to know your surroundings.

19. Be Patient:
   - Remember that unpacking and organizing take time. Be patient with yourself, and tackle one task at a time to avoid feeling overwhelmed.

Creating an organized and functional living space is a rewarding part of the moving process. By following these steps and taking your time, you'll transform your new house into a comfortable and welcoming home where you can truly settle in and enjoy your new life.

Personalizing Your New Home

One of the most exciting aspects of moving into a new home is the opportunity to personalize it and make it uniquely yours. Personalization allows you to infuse your personality, style, and preferences into your living space, creating a comfortable and inviting environment. Here are some tips on how to personalize your new home:

1. Take Your Time:
   - Personalizing your home is a journey, not a race. Take your time to understand the space and how you want it to feel. Avoid rushing into decisions that you may later regret.

2. Create a Vision:
   - Start by envisioning how you want your home to look and feel. Consider your personal style, color preferences, and the overall ambiance you want to achieve.

3. Choose a Color Palette:
   - Select a color palette that resonates with you and complements the space. Paint walls, add colorful decor items, or choose furniture and textiles that incorporate your chosen colors.

4. Display Personal Photos and Art:
   - Hang family photos, artwork, and memorabilia that hold sentimental value. These personal touches make your home feel warm and welcoming.

5. Mix Old and New:
   - Don't be afraid to mix old and new furniture and decor. Vintage or heirloom pieces can add character and history to your space.

6. Customize Furniture:
   - If possible, invest in custom-made furniture or upholstery to reflect your unique style and fit your space perfectly.

7. Consider Your Hobbies and Interests:
   - Showcase your hobbies and interests in your home's design. For example, if you love books, create a cozy reading nook. If you're a plant enthusiast, decorate with indoor plants.

8. Add Personal Decor:
   - Incorporate personal decor items like throw pillows, rugs, curtains, and lighting fixtures that resonate with your style.

9. DIY Projects:
   - Consider DIY projects to personalize your space further. Create handmade art, craft custom shelving, or refurbish furniture to make it your own.

10. Home Fragrance:
    - Use scents like candles, essential oils, or diffusers to add a personal fragrance to your home. Scents can evoke memories and create a cozy atmosphere.

11. Accessorize Thoughtfully:
    - Accessorize with items that have meaning to you. It could be a souvenir from a memorable trip, a family heirloom, or a unique find from a local artisan.

12. Personalize Bedrooms:
    - Customize bedrooms to reflect the personalities and interests of those who occupy them. Allow family members to choose decor elements that resonate with them.

13. Outdoor Spaces:
    - Personalize your outdoor spaces, such as the garden, patio, or balcony, with plants, outdoor furniture, and decor that create an inviting oasis.

14. Child's Playroom or Nursery:
    - Create a fun and imaginative playroom or nursery for children. Use themes, colors, and decor that inspire creativity and joy.

15. Home Office:
    - Personalize your home office with decor that inspires productivity and reflects your professional identity.

16. Rotate Decor:
    - To keep your space feeling fresh, periodically rotate and update decor items. This can breathe new life into your home without major renovations.

17. Engage Family and Friends:
    - Involve your family and friends in the process of personalizing your home. Their input and assistance can make it a collaborative and enjoyable experience.

18. Stay True to Yourself:
    - Ultimately, your home should reflect your personality and preferences. Don't be swayed by trends or the opinions of others if they don't align with your vision.

Personalizing your new home is a creative and fulfilling endeavor that allows you to turn a house into a reflection of your unique identity and lifestyle. Embrace the process, enjoy the journey, and savor the satisfaction of living in a space that truly feels like home.

Getting to Know Your Neighborhood

As you settle into your new home, taking the time to get to know your neighborhood can enhance your sense of belonging and help you build a strong connection with your community. Here are some steps to help you become acquainted with your new neighborhood:

1. Take Strolls:
   - Go for leisurely walks or bike rides around your neighborhood. This allows you to explore your surroundings at a relaxed pace and discover nearby parks, shops, and local attractions.

2. Introduce Yourself:
   - Don't hesitate to introduce yourself to your neighbors. A friendly hello or a brief chat can go a long way in establishing a sense of community.

3. Attend Neighborhood Events:
   - Keep an eye out for neighborhood events, gatherings, or block parties. Participating in these activities can be an excellent way to meet your neighbors and become part of the community.

4. Join Community Groups:
   - Look for community groups, clubs, or associations that align with your interests. Whether it's a gardening club, book club, or sports league, joining these groups can help you connect with like-minded neighbors.

5. Support Local Businesses:
   - Frequent local businesses like coffee shops, restaurants, and stores. Not only will you discover hidden gems, but you'll also contribute to the local economy and become a familiar face in the community.

6. Explore Nearby Services:
   - Identify essential services near your home, such as grocery stores, schools, healthcare facilities, and public transportation. Familiarize yourself with their locations and operating hours.

7. Visit Community Centers:
   - Many neighborhoods have community centers that offer recreational programs, classes, and events. Check out these centers to see what they have to offer.

8. Volunteer:
   - Get involved in local volunteer opportunities or charitable organizations. This is an excellent way to give back to your community while getting to know your neighbors.

9. Attend Local Meetings:
   - Attend neighborhood association meetings or town hall gatherings. These meetings provide valuable information about local issues, developments, and opportunities for community involvement.

10. Join Online Neighborhood Groups:
    - Many neighborhoods have online forums or social media groups where residents discuss local news, events, and concerns. Joining these groups can help you stay informed and connected.

11. Participate in School Activities:
    - If you have children attending local schools, participate in school-related activities and meetings.

This is a great way to meet other parents and become engaged in your child's education.

12. Explore Parks and Recreation:
   - Visit local parks, trails, and recreational facilities. These areas are not only great for exercise and relaxation but also for meeting other residents who share similar interests.

13. Stay Informed:
   - Stay informed about your neighborhood by reading local newspapers, newsletters, and websites. Understanding the issues and developments in your area can help you become an informed and engaged resident.

14. Safety and Security:
   - Get to know your local law enforcement and emergency services. Familiarize yourself with safety measures and community resources available in case of emergencies.

15. Attend Cultural and Community Events:
   - Attend cultural festivals, fairs, and other community events. These gatherings often showcase the diversity and vibrancy of your neighborhood.

16. Explore Public Transportation:
   - If you use public transportation, become familiar with bus routes, train stations, and schedules. Efficient transportation options can enhance your accessibility to the broader community.

17. Ask for Recommendations:
   - Ask your neighbors for recommendations on local services, from contractors and handymen to doctors and schools. They can provide valuable insights based on their experiences.

Getting to know your neighborhood takes time, but the effort is rewarding. By actively engaging with your community, you'll not only build meaningful connections but also contribute to the sense of unity and camaraderie that makes a neighborhood feel like home.

Chapter 10: Navigating Challenges and Celebrating Success

Congratulations! You've embarked on an incredible journey and achieved the milestone of home ownership. While this journey has been filled with excitement, personal growth, and new beginnings, it's also essential to recognize that home ownership can present challenges and unexpected twists along the way.

This final chapter is dedicated to helping you navigate the challenges that may arise during your home ownership journey while celebrating the successes and triumphs you've experienced. home ownership is a significant achievement, and with it comes a sense of pride and responsibility. Let's explore how to tackle challenges with resilience and continue to thrive in your new home.

What to Expect in this Chapter:

In the following pages, we'll delve into various aspects of navigating challenges and celebrating success as a homeowner:

- Handling Unexpected Repairs: Strategies for dealing with unexpected home repairs and maintenance issues, from emergency fixes to long-term solutions.

- Financial Management: Tips for managing your budget, handling mortgage payments, and planning for future financial goals while owning a home.

- home ownership Milestones: Celebrate milestones and achievements in your home ownership journey, whether it's paying off your mortgage, completing a major renovation, or hosting memorable gatherings.

- Community Engagement: Explore ways to become an active and engaged member of your community, from volunteering to participating in neighborhood events.

- Resilience and Adaptation: Learn how to adapt to changing circumstances, overcome setbacks, and maintain a positive outlook as a homeowner.

- Reflection and Gratitude: Take time to reflect on your journey, express gratitude for your accomplishments, and set new goals for the future.

As you read through this chapter, remember that challenges are part of the home ownership experience. With the right mindset, preparation, and a resilient spirit, you can overcome obstacles and continue to enjoy the benefits of owning a place you can truly call home. Let's embark on this final part of your journey together.

Dealing with Unexpected Issues

home ownership comes with its share of unexpected challenges and issues. From sudden maintenance problems to unforeseen financial burdens, it's essential to be prepared to address these issues effectively. Here are some strategies to help you navigate unexpected challenges as a homeowner:

1. Emergency Fund:
   - Establish an emergency fund specifically for home-related expenses. This fund can cover unexpected repairs, such as a leaking roof or a broken furnace, without disrupting your overall financial stability.

2. Regular Maintenance:
   - Implement a routine maintenance schedule for your home. Regularly inspect and service essential systems, such as HVAC, plumbing, and electrical. Preventive maintenance can help identify issues before they become emergencies.

3. DIY Skills:
   - Develop basic do-it-yourself (DIY) skills for minor home repairs. Learning to fix small issues like a leaky faucet or a running toilet can save you money on service calls.

4. Research Contractors:
   - Identify reputable contractors, plumbers, electricians, and other professionals in your area. Establish a relationship with them before you need their services, so you have reliable contacts when emergencies arise.

5. Home Warranty:

- Consider purchasing a home warranty that covers major appliances and systems. This can provide financial protection against unexpected repair costs.

6. Insurance Coverage:
   - Review your homeowners insurance policy to understand what types of damage and repairs are covered. Ensure you have adequate coverage for potential risks like natural disasters.

7. Prioritize Repairs:
   - When facing multiple repairs or maintenance tasks, prioritize them based on urgency and safety. Address critical issues first to prevent further damage or safety hazards.

8. Get Multiple Quotes:
   - When seeking professional help for repairs or renovations, obtain multiple quotes to ensure you're getting fair pricing and quality workmanship.

9. Home Inspection:
   - If you're buying a home, consider investing in a comprehensive home inspection before the purchase. This can uncover potential issues that might not be apparent during a casual viewing.

10. Stay Informed:
    - Keep up with home improvement trends and technologies. New innovations may offer solutions to common household problems.

11. Budget for Home Repairs:
    - Include home repair and maintenance costs in your annual budget. Allocate a portion of your income to a dedicated home maintenance fund.

12. Ask for Advice:
    - Seek advice and guidance from experienced homeowners or mentors. They can share their wisdom and insights on dealing with unexpected issues.

13. Be Resilient:
    - Maintain a resilient mindset when facing home-related challenges. Remember that home ownership is a long-term commitment, and setbacks are a natural part of the journey.

14. Know When to Seek Help:
    - Don't hesitate to seek professional help when a problem is beyond your capabilities. Attempting complex repairs without expertise can lead to more significant issues.

15. Document Everything:
    - Keep records of all home-related expenses, repairs, and maintenance. This documentation can be useful for insurance claims, tax purposes, and future reference.

Dealing with unexpected issues is an inherent part of home ownership. By being proactive, financially prepared, and resourceful, you can effectively handle these challenges and ensure that your home remains a safe and comfortable haven for you and your family. Remember that each problem solved is an opportunity to enhance your skills and resilience as a homeowner.

Building Community and Relationships

Becoming an active and engaged member of your community not only enriches your home ownership experience but also creates a sense of belonging and support. Building strong relationships with your neighbors and participating in local activities can enhance your overall quality of life. Here are some tips on how to build community and foster relationships in your neighborhood:

1. Introduce Yourself:
   - Take the initiative to introduce yourself to your neighbors when you move in. A friendly greeting and a simple conversation can set the stage for positive relationships.

2. Attend Neighborhood Events:
   - Participate in neighborhood events, gatherings, or block parties. These occasions provide excellent opportunities to meet your neighbors in a relaxed and social setting.

3. Join Community Groups:
   - Look for local clubs, groups, or associations that align with your interests. Whether it's a homeowners' association, a gardening club, or a neighborhood watch, joining these groups can help you connect with like-minded residents.

4. Volunteer:
   - Seek out volunteer opportunities in your community. Whether it's helping with a neighborhood clean-up, organizing a charity drive, or participating in a local event, volunteering is a meaningful way to give back and connect with others.

5. Children's Activities:
   - If you have children, encourage them to engage in local sports, clubs, or activities. Attend school events and parent-teacher meetings to get involved in your child's education and meet other parents.

6. Join Online Community Groups:
   - Many neighborhoods have online forums, social media groups, or neighborhood-specific apps. Join these platforms to stay informed about local news, events, and community discussions.

7. Support Local Businesses:
   - Frequent local businesses and shops. Not only does this support your local economy, but it also allows you to meet other residents who share a commitment to the community.

8. Organize Events:
   - Consider hosting a gathering or event at your home. It could be a neighborhood barbecue, a holiday party, or a game night. Hosting events can help you connect with neighbors and create a sense of unity.

9. Engage in Neighborhood Improvement Projects:
   - Collaborate with your neighbors on projects that enhance the neighborhood, such as community gardens, street clean-ups, or beautification efforts.

10. Practice Good Neighborliness:
    - Be a considerate and respectful neighbor. Follow local noise ordinances, maintain your property, and offer assistance when needed.

11. Attend Local Meetings:

- Attend neighborhood association meetings or town hall gatherings. These meetings provide insight into local issues, developments, and opportunities for community involvement.

12. Be Approachable:
  - Be approachable and open to forming relationships with your neighbors. A welcoming demeanor can encourage others to reach out to you.

13. Celebrate Milestones:
  - Celebrate life milestones and achievements with your neighbors. Whether it's a birthday, a new baby, or a promotion, sharing these moments fosters a sense of community.

14. Offer Help:
  - Extend a helping hand when you see a neighbor in need. Whether it's shoveling snow, running errands, or lending tools, acts of kindness build strong bonds.

15. Be Inclusive:
  - Make an effort to include neighbors of different backgrounds, cultures, and generations in community activities. Embrace diversity and foster an inclusive environment.

Building community and relationships in your neighborhood enriches your home ownership experience by creating a supportive and welcoming environment. It also ensures that your home is not just a physical space but a place where you truly belong and thrive. By actively engaging with your neighbors and participating in local activities, you'll contribute to the strength and vibrancy of your community.

Achieving Your Long-Term home ownership Goals

As a homeowner, you've made a significant investment in your future. To make the most of your investment and achieve long-term home ownership success, it's crucial to set and work towards your goals. Whether you aim to pay off your mortgage, increase the value of your home, or create a comfortable retirement nest egg, here are strategies to help you achieve your long-term home ownership goals:

1. Create a Financial Plan:
  - Develop a comprehensive financial plan that outlines your home ownership goals, including paying off your mortgage, saving for home improvements, and building a retirement fund.

2. Mortgage Repayment Strategy:
  - Determine a mortgage repayment strategy that aligns with your long-term goals. Options include making extra payments, refinancing to lower interest rates, or switching to a shorter loan term.

3. Home Improvements:
  - Identify home improvement projects that can increase your property's value and enhance your living experience. Prioritize these projects based on your budget and goals.

4. Regular Maintenance:
  - Commit to ongoing home maintenance to prevent costly repairs in the future. A well-maintained home not only retains its value but also ensures a comfortable living environment.

5. Emergency Fund:

- Maintain an emergency fund specifically for home-related expenses. This fund can cover unexpected repairs, insurance deductibles, and other home ownership emergencies.

6. Savings and Investments:
   - Diversify your savings and investments to include real estate, retirement accounts, stocks, and bonds. Consult with a financial advisor to create a well-rounded investment portfolio.

7. Energy Efficiency:
   - Invest in energy-efficient upgrades, such as insulation, solar panels, and energy-efficient appliances. These improvements can reduce utility costs and increase the value of your home.

8. Monitor Property Value:
   - Stay informed about your property's value by regularly checking real estate market trends and assessing the value of comparable homes in your area.

9. Retirement Planning:
   - Consider how your home factors into your retirement plans. It can serve as a source of equity to fund retirement, a downsized living space, or a rental property for supplemental income.

10. Review and Adjust:
    - Periodically review your financial plan and home ownership goals. Life circumstances may change, requiring adjustments to your strategy.

11. Consult Professionals:
    - Seek advice from financial advisors, real estate professionals, and tax experts. Their expertise can help you make informed decisions that align with your long-term goals.

12. Downsizing or Upgrading:
    - Evaluate your long-term housing needs. Depending on your goals and lifestyle changes, you may consider downsizing to a smaller home, upgrading to accommodate a growing family, or exploring investment properties.

13. Stay Informed:
    - Stay informed about tax incentives, deductions, and credits related to home ownership. Taking advantage of these benefits can help you achieve your financial goals.

14. Pay Attention to Interest Rates:
    - Keep an eye on interest rates and consider refinancing your mortgage when favorable opportunities arise to lower your monthly payments or shorten the loan term.

15. Consult with Legal Professionals:
    - In estate planning, consider consulting with legal professionals to address property inheritance and the distribution of assets to heirs.

Long-term home ownership goals require careful planning, discipline, and adaptability. By setting clear objectives and following a well-structured financial plan, you can make your home an essential part of your financial success. Whether your goals involve financial security, retirement, or real estate investment, your home can play a pivotal role in achieving them.

Celebrating Your home ownership Journey

Your journey to home ownership has been filled with excitement, challenges, and personal growth. Now that you've settled into your new home and established a sense of stability, it's time to pause and celebrate your achievements. home ownership is a significant milestone, and acknowledging your journey can be a rewarding experience. Here are some ways to celebrate your home ownership journey:

1. Home Dedication Ceremony:
   - Host a home dedication ceremony or housewarming party to invite friends and family to share in your joy. It's a great opportunity to showcase your new home and create lasting memories.

2. Home Tour:
   - Invite loved ones for a tour of your home. Share stories about the process of finding and buying your home, as well as your plans for the future.

3. Create a Memory Book:
   - Document your home ownership journey in a memory book or scrapbook. Include photos, notes, and mementos that capture the milestones and memories along the way.

4. Personalize Your Space:
   - Continue personalizing your home with decor that reflects your style and values. Embrace each opportunity to make your home feel uniquely yours.

5. Reflect and Express Gratitude:
   - Take a moment to reflect on the journey and express gratitude for the support of family, friends, and professionals who helped you achieve your goal.

6. Family Traditions:
   - Establish new family traditions or rituals in your new home. This could be a monthly family game night, Sunday brunches, or annual holiday celebrations.

7. Host Gatherings:
   - Use your home as a gathering place for special occasions, holidays, and celebrations. Hosting loved ones in your own space can be a source of joy and pride.

8. Outdoor Living:
   - If you have outdoor space, create an inviting area for outdoor activities and relaxation. Celebrate your home ownership with outdoor gatherings and events.

9. Explore Local Amenities:
   - Explore the local amenities, parks, and attractions near your new home. Get to know your neighborhood and enjoy the benefits it offers.

10. Community Involvement:
    - Get involved in your community through volunteering, supporting local businesses, or participating in neighborhood events. Contributing to your community can be a fulfilling way to celebrate your home ownership.

11. Home Improvement Projects:

- Plan and embark on home improvement projects that enhance your living experience and add value to your property. Completing these projects can be a rewarding celebration of your home.

12. Involve Loved Ones:
    - Share your home ownership journey with loved ones by involving them in decorating, gardening, or home improvement projects. These collaborative efforts can strengthen relationships.

13. Relax and Unwind:
    - Dedicate time to relax and unwind in your new home. Create a peaceful sanctuary where you can recharge and appreciate the tranquility of home ownership.

14. Set New Goals:
    - Use this milestone as an opportunity to set new goals for your home ownership journey. Consider what you want to achieve in the years ahead and map out a plan to reach those goals.

15. Express Your Creativity:
    - Embrace your creative side by tackling DIY projects or crafting home decor. Personalized creations can add character and meaning to your living space.

16. Celebrate Anniversaries:
    - Mark the anniversary of your home purchase or move-in date with a special celebration. Reflect on the progress you've made since that day.

17. Share Your Story:
    - Share your home ownership journey with others who may be on a similar path. Your experiences and insights can inspire and motivate those aspiring to become homeowners.

Celebrating your home ownership journey is a way to recognize your hard work, dedication, and the fulfillment of a significant life goal. Embrace the pride and sense of accomplishment that come with owning a home, and use this milestone as a source of inspiration for future endeavors. Your home is not just a physical space; it's a symbol of your achievements and the memories you'll create in the years to come.

Reflecting on Your Journey

Taking time to reflect on your home ownership journey can be a meaningful and insightful exercise. It allows you to appreciate how far you've come, learn from your experiences, and set your sights on the future. Here's a guide to help you reflect on your journey as a homeowner:

1. Gratitude:
    - Begin by expressing gratitude for the opportunity to become a homeowner. Recognize the support, resources, and hard work that made it possible.

2. Milestones and Achievements:
    - Reflect on the milestones and achievements you've reached since acquiring your home. These could include paying off a portion of your mortgage, completing home improvement projects, or achieving personal goals.

3. Challenges and Lessons:

- Consider the challenges and setbacks you encountered along the way. Reflect on the lessons you've learned from these experiences and how they've contributed to your growth.

4. Home Memories:
   - Recall the special memories you've created in your home. Think about gatherings, celebrations, and everyday moments that have added warmth and meaning to your space.

5. Personal Growth:
   - Reflect on how home ownership has contributed to your personal growth and development. Consider the skills you've acquired, such as budgeting, DIY projects, or property management.

6. Financial Progress:
   - Evaluate your financial progress as a homeowner. Have you paid down your mortgage, increased your home's value, or achieved your financial goals?

7. Community Connection:
   - Think about the connections you've made within your community. Have you formed meaningful relationships with neighbors, engaged in local activities, or contributed to community improvement?

8. Future Aspirations:
   - Set new goals and aspirations for your home ownership journey. What would you like to achieve in the years ahead? Consider your dreams for your home and your community involvement.

9. Home Improvement:
   - Review the home improvement projects you've completed or plan to undertake. Reflect on how these projects have transformed your living space and contributed to your comfort and satisfaction.

10. Lifestyle Changes:
    - Acknowledge any lifestyle changes that have occurred since becoming a homeowner. Have your priorities shifted, and how has your home adapted to accommodate those changes?

11. Resilience and Adaptation:
    - Consider how you've demonstrated resilience and adaptability in response to unexpected challenges or changes in your home ownership journey.

12. Share Your Reflections:
    - Share your reflections with loved ones, friends, or a supportive community. Discussing your journey can provide additional insights and strengthen your sense of accomplishment.

13. Celebrate Your Achievements:
    - Take time to celebrate your achievements, both big and small. Treat yourself to a special celebration or create a ritual that honors your home ownership journey.

14. Document Your Reflections:
    - Write down your reflections in a journal, blog, or digital document. Documenting your journey allows you to revisit your thoughts and insights in the future.

15. Set New Goals:
    - Based on your reflections, set new goals for your home ownership journey. What do you want to

accomplish in the coming months or years? Create a plan to work toward those goals.

16. Express Gratitude Again:
   - End your reflection with another expression of gratitude for the opportunity to own a home and shape your living environment.

Reflecting on your home ownership journey is an opportunity to acknowledge your achievements, embrace personal growth, and set a course for future success. It reminds you that your home is more than just a physical space; it's a canvas on which you can paint the story of your life and aspirations.

Planning for Your Future in Your New Home

As you settle into your new home, it's essential to plan for your future, both within the walls of your house and beyond. Your home can play a significant role in shaping your future, from financial stability to personal fulfillment. Here are some steps to help you plan for your future while enjoying the comforts of your new home:

1. Financial Goals:
   - Review your financial situation and establish clear financial goals. Consider your mortgage payments, savings, investments, and retirement plans. Create a budget that allows you to save for your future while maintaining your current lifestyle.

2. Emergency Fund:
   - Continue building and maintaining an emergency fund to cover unexpected expenses. Having financial security will provide peace of mind as you plan for the future.

3. Retirement Planning:
   - Evaluate your retirement savings and retirement age goals. Explore retirement accounts, such as 401(k)s and IRAs, and contribute regularly to secure your financial future.

4. Home Equity:
   - Recognize the potential of your home equity as an asset. Consider how it can be used for future financial needs, such as education expenses, home renovations, or supplemental income in retirement.

5. Property Investment:
   - Explore opportunities for property investment, such as purchasing rental properties or real estate investment trusts (REITs). Diversifying your investment portfolio can help secure your financial future.

6. Home Improvements:
   - Plan for home improvements that enhance your living experience and add value to your property. Invest in projects that align with your long-term goals, such as energy-efficient upgrades or renovations that increase your home's resale value.

7. Estate Planning:
   - Consider your estate planning needs, including creating or updating your will, establishing trusts, and designating beneficiaries. Ensure your property and assets are distributed according to your wishes.

8. Education Savings:
   - If you have children, plan for their education expenses by setting up education savings accounts or

529 plans. Saving for their future education will relieve financial stress when the time comes.

9. Career Development:
   - Reflect on your career goals and aspirations. Your home can be a conducive environment for remote work or entrepreneurship. Consider how your home can support your professional growth.

10. Health and Wellness:
    - Prioritize your health and wellness by creating a space in your home for fitness, relaxation, and healthy living. Investing in your well-being now can lead to a healthier and more fulfilling future.

11. Community Engagement:
    - Continue to engage with your community through volunteering, local events, and social activities. Building strong community connections can contribute to a fulfilling and enriched future.

12. Long-Term Home Adaptations:
    - Plan for any future adaptations your home may require as you age. Consider accessibility features, such as ramps, grab bars, and wider doorways, to ensure your home remains suitable for your needs.

13. Sustainable Living:
    - Embrace sustainability and energy efficiency in your home to reduce long-term utility costs and environmental impact. Sustainable choices today can lead to a more sustainable future.

14. Downsizing or Upsizing:
    - Assess your long-term housing needs. Depending on lifestyle changes, you may need to downsize or upsize your home. Plan for these transitions based on your future goals.

15. Travel and Experiences:
    - Incorporate travel and experiences into your future plans. Your home can serve as a base for adventures and memorable journeys, so allocate resources to fulfill your travel dreams.

16. Continuous Learning:
    - Invest in continuous learning and personal development. Consider dedicating space in your home for reading, studying, or pursuing hobbies and interests that contribute to your growth.

Planning for your future in your new home involves a holistic approach that considers financial stability, personal growth, and overall well-being. Your home is not just a place to live; it's a foundation upon which you can build a brighter future. By setting clear goals and taking proactive steps, you can enjoy the comforts of your home while confidently moving toward a fulfilling and prosperous future.

Paying It Forward: Helping Others on Their Path to home ownership

As a homeowner who has successfully navigated the journey to owning your own space, you have the opportunity to make a meaningful impact on others who aspire to achieve the same dream. Paying it forward by helping others on their path to home ownership is not only a way to give back to your community but also a way to share the knowledge and experiences you've gained. Here are ways you can offer guidance and support to those pursuing home ownership:

1. Share Your Story:
   - Start by sharing your own home ownership journey. Talk about the challenges you faced, the

strategies you used, and the milestones you reached. Your personal story can inspire and motivate others.

2. Mentorship:
   - Offer to mentor individuals or families who are considering home ownership. Provide guidance on the process, share valuable insights, and answer their questions.

3. Educational Workshops:
   - Host workshops or informational sessions in your community on various aspects of home ownership, such as budgeting, credit management, and homebuying tips. Invite experts to speak and share their expertise.

4. Volunteer with Housing Organizations:
   - Volunteer your time with local housing organizations and nonprofits that support affordable housing initiatives. Your assistance can make a significant difference in helping others secure safe and stable homes.

5. Financial Counseling:
   - Offer financial counseling or coaching to individuals seeking to improve their financial situation in preparation for home ownership. Help them create budgets and savings plans.

6. Homebuyer Seminars:
   - Organize or participate in homebuyer seminars where you can provide practical advice and answer questions about the homebuying process.

7. Connect with Real Estate Professionals:
   - Establish connections with real estate agents, lenders, and housing experts in your area. You can refer aspiring homebuyers to trusted professionals who can guide them through the process.

8. Support Affordable Housing Initiatives:
   - Advocate for affordable housing initiatives in your community. Participate in discussions, attend meetings, and support policies that promote home ownership opportunities for all.

9. Network with Local Resources:
   - Familiarize yourself with local resources, grants, and programs that assist first-time homebuyers or those with limited income. Share this information with those in need.

10. Assist with Down Payment:
    - If possible, consider providing financial assistance or loans for down payments to friends or family members who are ready to buy their first home.

11. Home Tours:
    - Offer to take prospective buyers on tours of your own home. Sharing your experience as a homeowner can provide valuable insights into what to look for when purchasing a property.

12. Create a Support Group:
    - Establish a support group or community forum where aspiring homebuyers can connect, share experiences, and seek advice from those who have already achieved home ownership.

13. Emphasize Responsible Ownership:
   - Stress the importance of responsible home ownership, including the commitment to maintaining and caring for one's property, being a good neighbor, and contributing positively to the community.

14. Celebrate Success Stories:
   - Recognize and celebrate the successes of those who have achieved home ownership with your support. Highlight their stories as inspiration for others.

15. Stay Informed:
   - Continue to educate yourself about changes in the real estate market, financing options, and home ownership trends. Staying informed allows you to provide up-to-date advice.

16. Encourage Saving:
   - Encourage aspiring homebuyers to establish savings goals and create a dedicated savings plan for their down payment and closing costs.

Paying it forward by helping others on their path to home ownership can have a lasting impact on individuals and families in your community. By sharing your knowledge, resources, and support, you can empower others to achieve the dream of home ownership and contribute to the strength and stability of your neighborhood. Your guidance can be a beacon of hope for those embarking on their own home ownership journey.

Here is a comprehensive list of hints and tips for first-time homebuyers:

1. Set Clear Financial Goals:
   - Determine your budget and financial goals for home ownership, including down payment, monthly mortgage payments, and other associated costs.

2. Improve Your Credit Score:
   - Prioritize improving your credit score before applying for a mortgage. A higher credit score can lead to better loan terms and lower interest rates.

3. Save for a Down Payment:
   - Start saving for a down payment early to secure favorable mortgage terms. Consider assistance programs for first-time buyers.

4. Build an Emergency Fund:
   - Maintain an emergency fund to cover unexpected expenses related to home ownership, such as repairs or unexpected job loss.

5. Research Loan Options:
   - Explore various mortgage options, including fixed-rate, adjustable-rate, FHA, VA, and USDA loans. Choose the one that best fits your financial situation.

6. Get Pre-Approved:
   - Obtain mortgage pre-approval before house hunting to know your budget and strengthen your offer when you find the right home.

7. Understand Closing Costs:

- Familiarize yourself with the closing costs, which include fees for appraisal, title search, and attorney services. Budget for these expenses.

8. Prioritize Location:
   - Consider the location carefully, taking into account proximity to work, schools, amenities, and safety.

9. Research Neighborhoods:
   - Investigate neighborhoods by visiting at different times of the day and talking to residents. Check local crime rates and schools.

10. Attend Open Houses:
    - Attend open houses in your desired area to get a feel for different homes and their features.

11. Hire a Real Estate Agent:
    - Choose an experienced real estate agent who understands your needs and can guide you through the buying process.

12. Negotiate Wisely:
    - Be prepared to negotiate the price and terms of your offer. Your real estate agent can assist you in this process.

13. Home Inspection:
    - Always schedule a professional home inspection to uncover any hidden issues or needed repairs before finalizing the purchase.

14. Home Appraisal:
    - Understand that your lender will require a home appraisal to ensure the property's value matches the loan amount.

15. Home Insurance:
    - Secure homeowner's insurance before closing on your home to protect against unforeseen events.

16. Review the HOA:
    - If the property is part of a homeowners' association (HOA), review its rules, fees, and regulations before committing.

17. Calculate All Costs:
    - Calculate the full cost of home ownership, including property taxes, insurance, maintenance, and utilities.

18. Reserve for Home Maintenance:
    - Set aside funds for ongoing home maintenance and repairs, typically around 1-3% of your home's value annually.

19. Get Multiple Quotes:
    - Obtain multiple quotes for services such as home inspections, insurance, and closing costs to ensure you get the best deals.

20. Be Patient:
   - Be patient and do not rush into a decision. Take your time to find the right home that meets your needs and budget.

21. Inspect the Neighborhood:
   - Investigate the neighborhood's noise level, traffic patterns, and amenities to ensure they align with your preferences.

22. Check the Resale Value:
   - Consider the resale potential of the property, as your housing needs may change in the future.

23. Read the Fine Print:
   - Carefully review all contracts, agreements, and disclosures related to the purchase of the property.

24. Plan for Future Growth:
   - Think about your future needs, such as a growing family or potential job changes, and whether the property can accommodate them.

25. Think Long Term:
   - Approach home ownership as a long-term investment and be prepared to commit to your home for several years.

26. Learn About Taxes:
   - Understand the tax implications of home ownership, including potential deductions and credits.

27. Energy Efficiency:
   - Look for energy-efficient features in your home, such as insulation, appliances, and windows, to reduce utility costs.

28. Document Everything:
   - Keep thorough records of all documents and transactions related to your home purchase for future reference.

29. Seek Professional Advice:
   - Consult with a financial advisor, attorney, or real estate expert to ensure you make informed decisions.

30. Trust Your Instincts:
   - Trust your instincts when making decisions about the home you want to buy. If something doesn't feel right, explore other options.

31. Plan for the Unexpected:
   - Have a contingency plan for unforeseen events, such as job loss or health issues, that may affect your ability to meet mortgage payments.

32. Read Reviews:
   - Check online reviews and ratings of real estate professionals, contractors, and home service providers before hiring them.

33. Utilities and Services:
   - Set up utilities, services, and internet in your new home before moving in to ensure a smooth transition.

34. Home Security:
   - Invest in home security measures to protect your property and loved ones.

35. Home Warranty:
   - Consider purchasing a home warranty to cover major appliances and systems in your new home for added peace of mind.

36. Meet Your Neighbors:
   - Introduce yourself to your neighbors and build positive relationships with them.

37. Home Organization:
   - Develop a system for home organization to keep your living space clutter-free and functional.

38. Keep Records:
   - Maintain a home maintenance log and keep records of repairs, improvements, and warranties.

39. Stay Informed:
   - Stay updated on real estate market trends and regulations that may affect your property or finances.

40. Enjoy the Journey:
   - Embrace the adventure of home ownership, and remember that your new home is a place to create lasting memories and experiences.

Navigating the process of buying your first home can be overwhelming, but with careful planning, research, and support, you can make informed decisions and achieve your home ownership goals.

www.ingramcontent.com/pod-product-compliance
Lightning Source LLC
Chambersburg PA
CBHW082215220526
45470CB00010B/3181